# California F

## The Famous, Infamous, and Quirky
### of the Golden State

**Teri Davis Greenberg**

Camino Books, Inc.
Philadelphia

*To Jeff, my husband and first love,*
*and Jamie and Shane,*
*our own California firsts*

Manufactured in the United States of America

1 2 3 4 5   05 04 03 02

Library of Congress Cataloging-in-Publication Data

Greenberg, Teri Davis.
   California firsts : the famous, infamous, and quirky of the Golden State / Teri Davis Greenberg.
      p. cm.
Includes bibliographical references.
   ISBN 0-940159-61-9 (alk. paper)
  1. California—History—Miscellanea.  I. Title.
   F861.6.G74 2001
   979.4—dc21                                      00-012578

Many of the designations used by manufacturers and sellers to distinguish their products are claimed as trademarks. Where those designations appear in this book, and Camino Books, Inc., was aware of a trademark claim, the designations have been printed in caps or initial caps.

Cover and interior design: Jerilyn Kauffman

This book is available at a special discount on bulk purchases for promotional, business, and educational use.

*For information write:*
Camino Books, Inc.
P.O. Box 59026
Philadelphia, PA 19102

www.caminobooks.com

# CONTENTS

## ACKNOWLEDGMENTS

I wish to thank the following people for their help in the preparation of this volume: my father, Sam Davis, of Davis Marketing Communications—electrical engineer–turned–technical writer and computer whiz—for his down-to-earth explanations of the many high-tech subjects covered and for his numerous repairs to my computer during the course of writing this book; my husband, Jeff Greenberg, my mother, Marlene Davis, and my sister, Dana Lentz, for their encouragement and feedback during the writing process; my fellow writers and friends from the Writer's Café—Mike Johnson for reviewing and commenting on some of the articles; Eve Salczynski for cheering me on during the process; Warren Kirbo for his insightful comments pertaining to several articles as well as for "cleaning up" some of the photos; and Gordon Permann for his legwork in procuring the *Spirit of St. Louis* and Lindbergh photos from the San Diego Aerospace Museum. Thanks also go out to Steve Levine of Uncle Milton Industries; Erin Marshall of Knott's Berry Farm; Carolyn Cole of the Los Angeles Public Library; Lorraine Alkire of Mattel; Lorraine Crouse of the J. Willard Marriott Library Manuscripts Division, University of Utah; Alex "A. J." Lutz of the San Diego Aerospace Museum; Dave Linden of the Petersen Automotive Museum; Harrison Hartman of E.W. Bullard Co.; and the photographic collections staff of the Ronald Reagan Library. I also wish to thank Lissa Sanders, my editor-in-chief at Windsor Publications, who hired me straight out of college 20 years ago to be her editorial assistant. My 12 years of editorial and photo research experience at Windsor contributed greatly to my knowledge and love of state and local history and helped tremendously in the preparation of this volume. Finally, I thank the publisher of Camino Books, Edward Jutkowitz, for trusting me to write this book and editor Carol Hupping for recommending me to him.

**Teri Davis Greenberg**

First California's gold beckoned risk-takers in search of wealth and adventure. While some returned home disheartened and broke, others made a living, even a fortune, and chose to stay. For those without ties and those wishing to sever old ones, California provided the perfect haven. Its enviable climate, wide-open opportunity, and anonymity appealed to anyone looking for a new start.

With the completion of the transcontinental railroad, the creation of the automobile and the national highway system, and the inauguration of air passenger service, those seeking greener pastures and employment in cutting-edge industry headed for California. The migration that began in 1849 in search of "real" gold continues, as thousands arrive daily hoping to discover or create their own metaphorical gold.

The number of "firsts" to which the Golden State stakes claim is truly mind-boggling. This small book only skims the surface of California's mother lode of national and global firsts. The high-tech, biotech, tourist, entertainment, recreation, hospitality, agriculture, aerospace, and communications industries have all achieved firsts in California. Innovation, creativity, and genius have flourished in the spiritual and cultural realms as well, with the state giving the world some of its most charismatic religious leaders and most of its best-loved film stars.

Furthermore, because so many musical artists have either started or jump-started their careers in Southern California or the Bay Area, it would be unfair and impossible to highlight just a few. Therefore, to represent the state's musicians and songwriters, each chapter title is borrowed from a song title by an artist or group with ties to the state.

This book is meant to be entertaining and informative. Whether you pick and choose what to read or you devour the information in one sitting from cover to cover, I hope you'll come away with a smile on your face, thinking, "I didn't know that!" So, without further ado, I introduce you to *California Firsts: The Famous, Infamous, and Quirky of the Golden State.*

# "Reelin' in the Years"
## Historical Firsts

*"The Gold Rush shaped who Californians are as a people—risk takers, eccentrics and innovators—and how the rest of the world still perceives them."*

Paul Rogers, *San Jose Mercury News*

Never had so many people traveled so far over a relatively short period of time as they did following James Marshall's discovery of gold near Sacramento in 1848. Their destination—Northern California. Their motivation—quick wealth.

The first major gold rush in American history has left its legacy on California, its people, and the rest of the world. Several historians and writers consider the Gold Rush a defining moment in the state's history. California state librarian Kevin Starr commented, "The Gold Rush jump-started California into its American identity. It established the cultural DNA for the state. You cannot understand contemporary California without understanding the Gold Rush." In his PBS documentary *The Gold Rush*, writer and coproducer Mike Trinklein stated, "Suddenly California ushered in this idea that you could get rich quick. That idea is still part of the American fabric. Everyone in America has a get-rich-quick scheme to this day." Steve Wiegand of the *Sacramento Bee* has called gold

"California's birthstone." And historian J. S. Holliday has said of the Gold Rush's impact on the rest of the country:

> The California Gold Rush made America a more restless nation—changed the people's sense of their future, their expectations and their values. Suddenly there was a place to go where everyone could expect to make money quickly, where life could be freer, where one could escape the restraints and conventions and the plodding sameness of life in the Eastern states.

Not only was the Gold Rush a decisive factor in congressional approval for a transcontinental railroad as well as in determining its route, but it also sped up Far West settlement and hastened California's admission to the Union.

Millwright James Marshall never profited from the California Gold Rush. Tragically, he died a penniless alcoholic, as did John Sutter, his former boss. *From Hayward and Blanche Cirker,* Dictionary of American Portraits, *Dover, 1974.*

Thirty-seven-year-old carpenter and millwright James Marshall could not have anticipated the far-reaching impact his discovery would have on California, the nation, and the world. On January 24, 1848, while constructing a sawmill for John Sutter on the south fork of the American River in Coloma, Marshall noticed something sparkling in the millrace. He excitedly blurted out to his construction crew, "Hey boys, by God, I believe I've found a gold mine." In reality, Marshall had exposed the Mother Lode, a 120-mile-long vein of gold running from California's Mariposa to Grass Valley.

Though Marshall and Sutter tried to keep the find a secret until sawmill construction could be completed, the news spread quickly via word of mouth. Then, on March 15, *The Californian* newspaper of San Francisco (population 800) printed the first notice of the discovery. Most thought the story a hoax. In December 1848, however, 220 ounces of California gold arrived in Washington, D.C., and President James K. Polk confirmed the rumor as true.

When official news of Marshall's discovery traveled around the world, many countries were facing political, social, and economic upheaval coupled with drought and famine. Desperate for a new start, Europeans, Asians, South Americans, Mexicans, Pacific Islanders, Australians, and others looked to the California gold fields as a place of hope. In addition, U.S. Easterners and Midwesterners saw an opportunity to become rich. As gold fever gripped the country, many left their families, friends, jobs, and homes in search of riches.

In the mid-19th century there were only two ways to reach California—by land or by sea. Both involved long, hard, dangerous journeys. Nevertheless, in 1849 at least 32,000 people, the overwhelming majority of them men, made the trek by horseback, on foot, or by wagon. The following year, another 44,000 undertook the 2,200-mile trip from trailheads in Iowa or Missouri. Depending on the route chosen, the overland trip could take from about three to six months or more. Though many "Forty-Niners" died along the way, by 1854 more than 300,000 people had traveled to California (1 in 90 U.S. residents). The 1850 census showed that

92 percent of California's population was male, and 73 percent was between 20 and 40 years of age.

Ships brought some East Coast Americans and tens of thousands of foreigners not living on the North American continent. There were two sea routes—around Cape Horn or to Panama, followed by a three- or four-day trip by mule or canoe to the Pacific Ocean. From there, gold seekers would board another ship that would take them to San Francisco. After disembarking, the men would travel another 150 miles inland to reach the gold fields. In 1849, more than 500 ships traveled 15,000 miles and five months to reach California, and between April 1849 and January 1850 roughly 40,000 people arrived by sea in San Francisco. Shipboard conditions were abominable, with inadequate food and water, contagious disease, and severe storms. Shipwrecks were common.

Mining, as most men discovered, was difficult, monotonous, and dangerous work. Mining camps could also be hazardous to one's emotional and physical well-being. Many a miner found himself homesick, lonely, isolated, ill, injured, or malnourished. Violence was rampant in the mining camps, where vigilante justice ruled and suicide wasn't uncommon. To escape their rough-and-tumble existence, most miners took up gambling and heavy drinking, and many frequented prostitutes. According to some estimates, one in five miners who came to California in 1849 died within six months.

From 1848 until the end of the 1850s, California's miners found at least $595 million worth of gold, or about $12 billion worth in today's dollars. In the beginning years of the Gold Rush, a miner could make about $25 a day, but as the region became overrun with gold seekers, a day's earnings dropped to about $16 and then $6.

In 1849, San Francisco's population doubled every 10 days, and the state's population rose from 12,000 non–Native Americans in 1848 to 300,000 only six years later. The majority of those who struck it rich were entrepreneurs "mining the miners"—such as Levi Strauss (clothing), Domenico Ghirardelli (food), and Leland Stanford (railroad)—who supplied necessary goods and services to the mining population.

The Gold Rush ended in 1864, but its legacy lives on. Residents as well as outsiders view California as a place of possibility, where it is OK to take risks, fail, and start over again. Not unlike the Forty-Niners, today's gold seekers are looking for opportunity and freedom from convention, both abundant in the Golden State.

## The First Gold Rush

The nation's first gold rush, though not at all comparable to the one set off by Marshall's Northern California discovery, actually took place in Southern California's Santa Clarita Valley in 1842.

While searching for some stray horses, Francisco Garcia Lopez decided to take a siesta under an oak tree. While asleep, he had a dream in which he discovered gold. When he awoke from his nap, a hungry Lopez dug up some wild onions for lunch. In the dirt, he discovered a piece of gold. Continuing to dig, he found more.

As word spread of Lopez's find, locals rushed to the area and began extracting more of the precious metal. Between 1842 and 1844, miners took nearly $100,000 worth of gold. When news of the 1848 discovery reached Southern California, however, the miners took off for the north.

Then, in about 1855, mining resumed at the Lopez site. Working with a group of Native Americans, Francisco Garcia Lopez managed to take out $65,000 worth of gold in one season.

### TALK ABOUT INFLATION!

During the Gold Rush, prices were so inflated that only the luckiest miners could afford to eat out or buy new boots. Breakfast could run $6 (the equivalent of about $150 in today's dollars); eggs, $1 to $3 ($25 to $75); coffee, $5 a pound ($125); boots, about $50 a pair ($1,250).

## To Visit: Marshall Gold Discovery State Historic Park

The park, with a museum, Gold Rush exhibits, a replica of Sutter's Mill, historic buildings, and Marshall's gravesite, also offers visitors the opportunity to pan for gold.

### Marshall Gold Discovery State Historic Park

Located in Coloma on Highway 49 (named after the Forty-Niners) between Placerville and Auburn.

530-622-3470

Hours: Call before visiting.

Admission: A park use fee is charged. Fee includes museum admission.

## "OFFSHORE" OIL WELLS: BLACK GOLD FROM THE DEEP BLUE

The world's first offshore oil wells, once located along the shoreline of Summerland (between Carpinteria and Santa Barbara), began producing black gold more than a half-century before the first "modern" commercial offshore oil wells were drilled off the Louisiana coast.

From today's perspective, the Summerland oil field is considered "nearshore" instead of "offshore." In 1896, however, when oilmen drilled the wells to a depth of 300 feet below sea level, they became the first in the world to extract oil from the ocean floor. Unlike today's offshore wells that operate from platforms miles from land, the late-19th-century wells were drilled from wooden piers extending into the Pacific. They were actually an extension of Summerland's onshore oil fields and the onshore drilling technology of the time.

Before an oil boom ensued and derricks punctuated the Pacific shore and coastline, the population of Summerland comprised a unique group of residents—about 500 Spiritualists. When Easterner and Spiritualist Henry L. Williams settled the area (then known as Ortega) in 1883, he had plans to transform the tiny beach settlement into a Spiritualist

In 1896, the world's first off-shore oil wells were drilled from wooden piers that extended into the ocean off the shore of Summerland, near Santa Barbara. *Courtesy of Teri Davis Greenberg*

haven. He renamed the community "Summerland" after a Spiritualist book of that title.

In 1884, Williams built a large house with an ocean view, and five years later subdivided his ranch land into lots measuring 25 feet by 60 feet. He then sold the lots for $25 to his fellow Spiritualists, most of whom had journeyed to the area from England. Some built houses; others lived in tents. They wanted to be able to conduct their seances undisturbed, and Summerland seemed to be the perfect place. (Santa Barbara residents nicknamed the town "Spooksville.")

In 1895, while attempting to dig a water well on his lot, a Mr. Cole struck oil. Soon other Summerland residents also discovered oil on their properties. When word got out, wildcatters rushed to the area, eager to cash in on the boom. Unfortunately for the Spiritualists, their beautiful Pacific haven soon didn't look, feel, or smell the same. The wildcatters had drilled wells and erected derricks everywhere, including in the ocean, making the town and coastline an eyesore. Some outraged Santa Barbara residents, who were particularly upset by an unsightly derrick on Miramar Beach, razed the structure in the dark of night.

In 1899, Henry Williams died when he fell down one of his wells. His widow married well-to-do George F. Becker, who then bought up Williams's oil properties and started Summerland Oil Company. At one time, J. Paul Getty unsuccessfully tried to buy the company. But by the 1930s, the oil boom was over, and Summerland began to settle back into its less hectic pre-boom state.

## AMERICA'S FIRST SUCCESSFUL GENERAL STRIKE

*"General strike: stoppage of work by a substantial proportion of workers in each of a number of industries in an organized endeavor to achieve economic or political objectives."*

*Encyclopaedia Britannica,* 2000

The general strike that paralyzed San Francisco for four days during the Great Depression resulted in what is considered the first "successful" general strike in the history of American labor.

The events leading up to the 1934 general strike had begun 15 years earlier, on the heels of World War I, when the International Longshoremen's Association (ILA) was stripped of its power in dealing with shipowners, which resulted in the exploitation and unethical treatment of longshoremen. There were the dreaded shape up, a San Francisco institution in which dock workers lined up each morning hoping to be chosen by a gang boss who expected various favors (bribes) in exchange

A San Francisco police officer prepares to club a striker during the 1934 general strike in San Francisco, the first "successful" general strike in the United States. *Courtesy of the National Archives, Still Pictures Branch*

for work; the fink hall (in other ports), a type of indoor shape up that was run by the employers and utilized bribery tactics to procure work; and an employer-run "union" called the Longshoremen's Association of San Francisco, also known as the Blue Book Union because only workers carrying a little blue book would be given work. In reality, the existence of a Longshoremen's Association was an attempt to prevent the formation of a worker-run union. To make matters worse, the gang bosses of San Francisco's Dollar Steamship Company hired only dock workers who promised to kick back 10 percent of their wages. (In 1933, a San Francisco longshoreman earned 75 cents an hour.)

With 50 percent of longshoremen on the relief rolls in 1933, Section 7(a) of the National Industrial Recovery Act, which guaranteed the right to unionize, gave these workers the hope of rebuilding the ILA. With intolerable working conditions and not enough work to go around, a Communist-produced newsletter called *The Waterfront Worker* disseminated among the rank and file led to a meeting of West Coast longshoremen in San Francisco in February 1934. The purpose of the convention was to reinvigorate the ILA, and the delegates produced a list of key demands: sharing the available work equitably through a union-controlled hiring hall, a one-dollar-per-hour wage, coastwide bargaining, and a 6-hour day and 30-hour week. The employers rejected the demands.

After numerous delays, including pleas from President Franklin D. Roosevelt to remain on the job, on May 9, 1934, 12,000 longshoremen went on strike in San Francisco and every port on the West Coast. Their goal was to "establish the rights of thousands of men to strike, to picket, to control their organization, to protect their unions, to raise wages and improve working conditions." Within a couple of weeks, about 10,000 seafaring-union members had also joined the strike. Then Teamsters union members in San Francisco, Oakland, Los Angeles, and Seattle voted to boycott the waterfront, refusing to move goods to or from the docks. On June 19, 1934, for the first time in the 20th century, no ships sailed into San Francisco Bay.

The national ILA president, without the approval of the rank and file, accepted two offers made by the shipowners, but the union members rejected both. Frustrated by their own national leadership and urged on by members of the newly organized Joint Marine Strike Committee, composed of five members from each of 10 unions, workers began considering a general strike. The events of July 5, 1934, proved to be the last straw. Known as Bloody Thursday, the day resulted in a riot in which police wielded clubs and shot at a crowd of 6,000 strikers, who retaliated by throwing bricks and dumping cargo from trucks. Two men, longshoreman Howard Sperry and strike supporter Nick Bordoise, were killed, and hundreds were injured. The riot halted construction on the San Francisco–Oakland Bay Bridge, and that evening the National Guard marched into San Francisco and the governor declared martial law along the Embarcadero.

On July 9, about 20,000 silent men, women, and children moved slowly down San Francisco's Market Street in a funeral procession for Sperry and

Bordoise. The bodies of the two men were carried aboard flatbed trucks ahead of the procession. The police were nowhere in sight.

On July 16, 1934, to protest the killings and the militia along the waterfront, the ILA called a general strike. All business and industry within San Francisco, except for utilities and the press, shut down. All restaurants closed except for a few sanctioned by the strikers. Nearly all teamsters ceased working except those delivering supplies to strikers and supporters. Streetcars did not run. Grocery store windows displayed signs stating "Closed Until the Boys Win." Teamsters blocked the only roads allowing access to the city. Pickets even took to the harbor on speedboats.

During the four-day strike, 7,000 National Guardsmen as well as law enforcement officers and "citizens" committees aligned themselves against unarmed strikers. Armed vigilantes attacked strikers and destroyed their meeting places.

Finally, on July 19, 1934, after the rank and file reviewed and approved a new arbitration offer, the Joint Marine Strike Committee accepted the offer. In San Francisco and other West Coast ports, all longshoremen, seamen, warehousemen, and other marine union workers lined up side by side and walked to the docks together. Showing union solidarity, they resumed work simultaneously.

The strike that began in May and culminated in the four-day general strike in July eventually involved more than 100,000 strikers and cooperative sympathizers. It resulted in improved hiring practices, better working conditions, and more control for workers over their lives. The shape up

### UNLIKELY SCABS

The coach of the football team at the University of California at Berkeley volunteered his players as strikebreakers during the longshoremen's strike. He told them the physical labor would be good training for the upcoming season.

and fink halls became things of the past as the new joint employer-and-union-run hall, staffed by a union dispatcher, brought union members the power they had fought for during the strike.

## FIRST AMERICAN CONCENTRATION CAMP: SHAME ON U.S.

Shortly after the bombing of Pearl Harbor, more than 120,000 law-abiding Japanese Americans living in the western United States were evacuated from their homes, forced to give up their businesses and property, and told to report to the nearest Civil Control Station. Once there, they were registered, numbered, tagged with shipping labels, and placed on buses, trains, or trucks under armed guard and brought to temporary detention facilities.

A dye works in Los Angeles's Little Tokyo made it clear to its patrons that they should pick up their clothing before shipping off to the Manzanar War Relocation Center in the Owens Valley. *Courtesy of the National Archives, Still Pictures Branch*

Upon arrival, they were body-searched, fingerprinted, interrogated, and assigned a space in a crudely built facility resembling a POW camp. They remained in this temporary camp for anywhere from two to seven months before being transported to a more permanent one, where they spent the next few years.

What had begun as wartime hysteria justified by what the federal government referred to as "military necessity" quickly turned into what the ACLU has called "the greatest deprivation of civil rights by government in this country since slavery." The FBI and the State Department had already completed a covert investigation of the Japanese American population and concluded that it did not pose a threat to national security. Despite these findings, Commander in Chief Franklin D. Roosevelt signed Executive Order 9066 on February 19, 1942 (against the advice of U.S. Attorney General Francis Biddle and FBI director J. Edgar Hoover), thus opening the most shameful chapter in U.S. history.

The carefully worded executive order authorized mass expulsion and incarceration of U.S. residents and citizens who might pose a security threat to the nation. It did not mention any specific ethnic group, but immediately following the attack on Pearl Harbor, California governor Culbert Olson and California's attorney general, Earl Warren, had demanded the removal of all Japanese Americans from the state. (Earl Warren later served as chief justice of the U.S. Supreme Court.)

Between February 25 and 27, 1942, California became the first state to execute the president's order when, under the command of Lieutenant General John L. DeWitt, the entire Japanese American community on Terminal Island (in Los Angeles County's San Pedro Bay area) was expelled.

By March 11, DeWitt had created the Wartime Civil Control Administration (WCCA) and placed Colonel Karl R. Bendetsen in command of the expulsion/detention plan. DeWitt used the "military necessity" rationale even though infants, children, and bedridden elderly, none of whom could pose a threat to national security, were all shipped off to concentration camps.

Military police line up at Manzanar in April 1942, while the camp was still considered a temporary detention center. Within two months, Manzanar was designated the country's first concentration camp. *Courtesy of the National Archives, Still Pictures Branch*

Though 10,312 Japanese Americans left the area on their own, an average of 3,750 people a day were transported to the temporary detention centers. By June 6, 1942, all of the Japanese Americans in the western United States had either fled or been detained. By August 7 of that year, 92,785 Californians of Japanese ancestry found themselves in the custody of the U.S. government.

During the temporary-detention phase of the operation, the War Department built 10 large concentration camps for the detainees. The first such camp, Manzanar War Relocation Center, stood on dusty Department of Water and Power (DWP) land in the windy Owens Valley between Independence and Lone Pine, in Inyo County. Actually, Manzanar had been hastily constructed as one of the temporary detention centers and had begun receiving Japanese Americans on March 22, 1942. Three months later, the War Relocation Authority (WRA) appropriated the facility for use as one of its permanent camps.

Some people refer to Manzanar and the nine other World War II–era camps by their government-given designation of war relocation centers or camps. After all, they reason, the United States wouldn't have concentration camps within its borders. However, *Webster's 10th Collegiate Dictionary* defines *concentration camp* as "a camp where persons (as prisoners of war, political prisoners, or refugees) are detained or confined." The refusal to accept the fact that the United States constructed and ran "concentration camps" is due to our conception of Nazi concentration camps, which, in reality, were death camps. Neither Manzanar nor any of the other nine camps was a death camp, but they *were* concentration camps. According to records in the National Archives, even government officials referred to them as concentration camps.

In its first year of operation, Manzanar held over 10,000 internees, with 6,500 U.S. citizens among them. The living area comprised 36 blocks, with each block containing 15 or 16 wooden 120-by-20-foot barracks. Each of the barracks was divided into six one-room "apartments," measuring from 320 to 480 square feet, in which families resided together or single people lived with strangers. Individual blocks shared a mess hall, a laundry, and a bath house. Privacy was nonexistent.

Constructed of wooden planks nailed to studs and covered with tar paper, the barracks provided little shelter from the hot summers, cold winters, and nearly year-round dust storms. Internees slept on straw-filled mattress ticking, covering themselves with a single army blanket.

Eight guard towers manned by armed military policemen (MPs) surrounded the camp, as did barbed wire. Internees were told the guards were there for their own protection, but they knew better. The guards pointed their weapons inward, toward the barracks, and at night they focused searchlights on prisoners walking from their barracks to the latrine. In Lieutenant General DeWitt's own words:

> The Assembly Centers in the combat area are generally located in grounds surrounded by fences clearly defining the limits for the evacuees. In such places the perimeter of the camp will be guarded to prevent unauthorized departure of evacuees . . .
> Should an evacuee attempt to leave camp without permission, he will be halted, arrested, and delivered to camp police.

In December 1942, a riot broke out between internees and MPs when a rumor circulated that one of the Anglos working at the camp had stolen rationed sugar. Months of pent-up anger and frustration erupted as the Japanese Americans threw stones at the soldiers and tried to push a truck through the locked gate. MPs fired tear gas at the internees, but it dissipated in the wind, so soldiers resorted to deadly force. Two people were killed and 11 were wounded by Thompson submachine guns and 12-gauge shotguns.

No other violent incidents were reported as time went on, although some elderly internees took their own lives. Two or three years into the life of the camp, security became more lax. Some prisoners were even allowed to picnic on the grounds surrounding the camp.

Later, internees were allowed to leave the camp for good if they signed a loyalty oath and found sponsorship. The oath asked them to swear their unqualified allegiance to the United States and to serve in the U.S. military if drafted. Several internees signed the oath and left California for the Midwest and the East Coast. Out of the more than 10,000 original Manzanar internees, by the end of the war, 6,000 were gone (including 158

### *"NO-NO BOYS"*

Male internees who refused to sign the loyalty oath were referred to as No-No Boys because they said "No" to both serving in the U.S. armed forces and swearing allegiance to the United States. While some didn't sign because they feared death at the hands of the Japanese government if Japan ended up winning the war, others refused to sign because they would not serve a country where law-abiding citizens could be rounded up and placed in concentration camps based on their ethnicity.

Renowned photographer Dorothea Lange captured dusty, desolate Manzanar with her lens, ironically, on the eve of Independence Day 1942. *Courtesy of the National Archives, Still Pictures Branch*

who had perished at the camp). Some of the approximately 4,000 remaining internees refused to sign the oath for various personal reasons.

In its final years of operation, Manzanar began to look like a village or small town. A high school and a judo gym opened; Bank of America and the U.S. Postal Service both opened branches; Sears, Roebuck found a ready market for its catalog merchandise; and a large hospital operated on camp land.

In 1946, the Army Corps of Engineers bulldozed Manzanar. The question lingers, however, as to why it or the other camps remained even after the "military necessity" rationale was proved to be unfounded.

Thirty-five years after Manzanar was destroyed, the Commission of Wartime Relocation and Internment of Civilians (CWRIC) concluded that the incarceration of Japanese Americans was not a military necessity, but was a result of racism and opportunism. The commission recommended that all those forced into the camps receive redress and an apology. So far, while some former internees have been given reparations, others are still waiting.

## Children's Village

Manzanar's Children's Village, the only orphanage among the 10 camps, received its first 40 children on June 23, 1942. Within the next three years, 61 more arrived. Interviews with some of the surviving orphans depict Children's Village as a sad, lonely place nearly devoid of adult role models.

Before the army removed the orphans from their "homes" and sent them to Manzanar, most had lived at Los Angeles's Maryknoll Home for Japanese Children, the Shonien (Japanese Children's Home of Los Angeles), the Salvation Army's Japanese Children's Home in San Francisco, and other Japanese American orphanages up and down the West Coast. In addition, infants were sent from other concentration camps shortly after their unwed teenage mothers gave birth to them.

Even top Manzanar official Ralph P. Merritt considered the existence of the camp orphanage ludicrous. On Thanksgiving 1942, he wrote: "The morning was spent at the Children's Village with the 90 orphans who had been evacuated from Alaska to San Diego and sent to Manzanar because they might be a threat to national security. What a travesty [of] justice!"

### ☀ To Visit: Manzanar National Historic Site and Eastern California Museum

While it is hard for people to believe that concentration camps existed in the United States, it is not as difficult for most to accept one of the camps as a National Historic Site. On March 3, 1992, Congress designated Manzanar a historic site, but the City of Los Angeles owned the land. On April 26, 1992, the National Park Service took title of the historic site. The date is significant because the last Saturday in April marks the day of the annual Manzanar pilgrimage to honor the internees.

## Manzanar National Historic Site

Location: Just off U.S. Route 395, 12 miles north of Lone Pine and 5 miles south of Independence.

Before visiting, check out www.nps.gov/manz/

## Eastern California Museum

To learn more about Manzanar, call 760-878-0258 or 760-878-0364 to arrange a visit to the Eastern California Museum in Independence.

Eastern California Museum
155 North Grant Street
Independence, CA 93526

## MOVIE STAR ELECTED U.S. PRESIDENT—RONALD REAGAN

*"My father used to say that he didn't know how you could be president without having been an actor. And it is a role that you have to play, that the public expects certain behavior out of a President . . . And I think that, to a certain extent, he did approach it as a role and he understood how to play that role, which is something that not all Presidents do."*

Ronald Reagan Jr.
ABC News interview, 1998

Ronald Wilson Reagan, born to Nelle and Jack Reagan in Tampico, Illinois, on February 6, 1911, remained in the Midwest throughout his high school and college years before relocating to California in 1937 in search of motion-picture stardom. California soon became home, whether Reagan was making movies, serving as the state's governor, retreating to his ranch for some R&R while president, or retiring in the Los Angeles area.

Reagan, who credits his mother for sparking his love of acting, decided to pursue it as a career upon graduation from Eureka College in 1932.

In 1954, Ronald Reagan, future president of the United States, began hosting television's *General Electric Theater.* A spokesman for GE as well, Reagan traveled the country communicating with diverse groups of people and honing his public-speaking skills.
*Courtesy of the Ronald Reagan Presidential Library*

Hearing that radio might be a good way to break into the business, he hitch-hiked from station to station in search of a broadcasting job. Eventually, he literally talked his way into a position as sports announcer for WOC radio in Davenport, Iowa. This first job became a stepping stone to a better one—broadcasting Chicago Cubs games for NBC affiliate WHO in Des Moines.

In 1937, Reagan convinced his boss to send him to California to cover the Cubs' spring training. He had an ulterior motive. A female colleague at WHO with contacts at Warner Brothers had already arranged a screen test for him. The test led to a seven-year contract and a salary of $200 a week.

With double features standard, there was the "A" movie (the "star" vehicle) and the "B" movie (featuring relatively unknown actors). Luckily for Reagan, the 1930s were the heyday of the "B" movie, and he appeared in many of them. Though he was credited as "Dutch" Reagan in his earliest films (a nickname that his father had given him), Warner Brothers switched to using his given name for about 50 films.

Reagan's breakthrough performance came in 1940's *Knute Rockne, All American*, in which he played a college football player. The role was perfect for him. It was in this film that Reagan uttered what was probably his most famous line: "Win one for the Gipper!" After *Knute Rockne*, Reagan began appearing in "A" movies. He met actress Jane Wyman, and the two married in 1940. They had a daughter, Maureen, in 1941 and adopted a son, Michael, in 1945.

During World War II, Reagan, who had joined the U.S. Army's Organized Reserve Corps (later called the Army Reserve) in 1937 as a private, was assigned to the 1st Motion Picture Unit in California. There he made more than 400 training films and patriotic pictures under the command of Jack Warner. He was honorably discharged as Captain Ronald Reagan in 1943.

After the war, the American public's taste in films and actors seemed to have changed, and the film industry followed the trend. Reagan didn't fit the new Brando-type movie-star image, and roles became more and more difficult to come by. Unwilling to cut ties with the profession he loved, Reagan decided to run for president of the Screen Actors Guild (SAG). In 1947, he won the election and held that office for five consecutive terms, and in 1959 he was reelected.

When he first became SAG president, Reagan was called to testify before the House Un-American Activities Committee (HUAC). Immersed in union and California Democratic politics, Reagan had been under surveillance by the FBI for possible Communist Party connections. By the time he testified before the HUAC, though, the New Deal liberal had become an FBI informant and detested Communists. He had seen how the Communist Party had tried to control organized labor in the film industry. According to Stephen Vaughn's 1993 book *Ronald Reagan in Hollywood: Movies and Politics,* while Reagan did not name names in the public hearings, in private he did. After testifying, he became so concerned for his safety that he began carrying a pistol.

Though Jane Wyman sued Reagan for divorce in 1948, the following year he met actress Nancy Davis under somewhat strange circumstances. She had been receiving unwanted mail from Communist sympathizers and didn't know what to do about it. Someone suggested she talk to the SAG president to see what he could do. So began a longtime relationship and an incredible life together. On March 4, 1952, Reagan married Davis, and they soon had a daughter, Patti. Later the Reagans had a son they named Ron Jr.

Reagan accepted a job as host of television's *General Electric Theater* in 1954. More so than his film career, the GE connection prepared Reagan for state and national politics. As he traveled the country speaking on behalf of the company, he met Americans from all walks of life. This new job not only honed his public-speaking skills but also strengthened his interest in politics.

In 1962, Reagan changed his party affiliation from Democratic to Republican. Then, in 1964, he delivered a televised speech for Barry Goldwater called "A Time for Choosing." The speech, and Reagan's TV appearance, caught the attention of several wealthy California business-men looking for the perfect Republican gubernatorial candidate to defeat Democratic governor Pat Brown. They convinced Reagan to run for gov-ernor of California. Though his past as an actor could have been used against him, in California it was a definite asset. He had name recognition, and he looked good on television. Reagan won a landslide victory over Brown by almost a million votes.

Reagan served two terms as governor of California (1967–75). During his first term, he made a half-hearted and unsuccessful attempt to become the Republican presidential candidate.

Near the end of his second term as governor, Reagan and his wife pur-chased Rancho del Cielo in the Santa Ynez mountains near Santa Barbara. The 688-acre property, complete with a 106-year-old, 1,300-square-foot adobe house, was the Reagans' oasis. As Reagan stated in 1992, "We relax at the ranch, which if not Heaven itself, probably has the same ZIP code." (Later, as president, Reagan traveled to his California ranch several times a year.)

The year after he ended his second term as governor, Reagan launched a nationwide speaking tour to assess his chances of becoming president. Challenging Gerald Ford for the Republican nomination in 1976, he lost by a narrow margin. But on July 17, 1980, Reagan was nominated as the Republican candidate for president. That November, he won an overwhelming victory over Jimmy Carter, partially because of Carter's inability to settle a hostage situation in Iran. Ninety minutes after Reagan took office, word came that the American hostages, who were held for 444 days, had been released.

The former Hollywood actor and governor of California was sworn in as the 40th president of the United States on January 20, 1981, making him the first professional actor to hold the highest office in the land. After serving two terms, President Reagan retired to his house in Los Angeles and his ranch near Santa Barbara. In 1998, with the former president stricken by Alzheimer's disease and no longer able to frequent the ranch, Nancy Reagan sold it to the Young America's Foundation to use as a retreat site.

### ☀ To Visit: Ronald Reagan Presidential Library and Museum

Ronald Reagan Presidential Library and Museum
40 Presidential Drive
Simi Valley, CA 93065
800-998-7641
www.reaganlibrary.net
Hours: Daily, 10 A.M.-5 P.M.
Admission charged.

# "I Get Around"
## Transportation and Travel

### CABLE CARS: SAN FRANCISCO'S MOVING LANDMARKS

In 1873, mechanical genius Andrew Smith Hallidie invented the world's first successful cable car system in San Francisco, thus bringing much-needed relief to the horses that had previously powered the city's streetcars.

Born Andrew Smith in London in 1836 to Scottish parents, Smith followed in the tracks of his inventor father (also named Andrew Smith). The elder Smith, who had patented the process for making metal wire rope, made sure his son was educated in all things scientific and mechanical.

At the age of 13, the younger Smith gained practical experience in the mechanical field while working for his brother, a machinist and draftsman. But the combination of manual labor by day and schooling at night proved too exhausting for young Smith, and he fell ill. At the time, the elder Smith was planning a journey to the California gold fields to investigate their financial prospects. Thinking the warm, sunny climate might help his son recuperate, he brought him along.

Father and son arrived in San Francisco in 1852, but finding the gold diggings a bust, the elder Smith returned to England the following year. His son remained in California and changed his surname to Hallidie after his godfather and uncle, Sir Andrew Hallidie (physician to King William IV and Queen Victoria). Thus, Andrew Smith became Andrew Smith Hallidie.

Andrew Hallidie's Clay Street Railway Company officially opened for business on September 1, 1873. The first cable car ran between San Francisco's Kearny and Leavenworth Streets. *From Edgar M. Kahn,* Cable Car Days in San Francisco, *Stanford University Press, 1940.*

For nearly four years, Hallidie tried his luck at mining in the Northern California gold fields, but when it became evident that gold mining would not pan out for him, he returned to San Francisco and began manufacturing wire rope using his father's patented process.

In the late 1860s, combining his experience in mining and wire-rope fabrication, he invented the "Hallidie Ropeway or Tramway" for use in mountainous mining areas. This invention, which made possible the transportation of heavy ore and equipment over what writer Edgar M. Kahn called an "elevated endless traveling line," utilized another of Hallidie's inventions—a steel cable "with a tensile strength of 160,000 pounds per square inch." This cable could bend over itself with a round turn, straighten out, and then repeat the procedure at the same spot without breaking.

Hallidie's impetus to develop the cable car came in 1869 after he witnessed a particularly brutal accident involving a streetcar drawn by a team of horses. In a report to the Mechanics Institute of San Francisco, Hallidie explained his motivation for developing the cable car:

I was largely induced to think over the matter from seeing the difficulty and pain the horses experienced in hauling the cars . . . the driving being accompanied by the free use of the whip and voice, and occasionally by the horses falling and being dragged down the hill on their sides by the car loaded with passengers sliding on its track.

By 1870, A. S. Hallidie and Company was manufacturing a heavy-duty yet flexible cable at its factory at Mason and Chestnut Streets in San Francisco. Having already developed the mechanical workings of the cable car based on his "Hallidie Ropeway or Tramway," all Hallidie needed was money.

London-born engineer Andrew Smith Hallidie came with his father to the California gold fields as a teenager. After four years of gold mining, Hallidie went on to manufacture wire rope, create the Hallidie Ropeway for mining in mountainous areas, and develop the world's first passenger cable car. *From Edgar M. Kahn,* Cable Car Days in San Francisco, *Stanford University Press, 1940.*

In 1872, with the help of three skeptical friends and business associates—Joseph Britton, Henry L. Davis, and James Moffitt—Hallidie formed the Clay Street Railway Company. To raise the money for the franchise fee, Hallidie spent countless hours trying to convince San Francisco's wealthy citizenry to fund the project. He managed to obtain $40,000 in pledges, but collected only $28,000. He contributed his $20,000 savings; his three associates put in $40,000; and the Clay Street Bank loaned him $30,000, payable over 10 years at 10 percent interest. By May 1872, financial matters had been settled.

The franchise Hallidie had acquired would expire at midnight August 1, 1873, so he would have to demonstrate a working cable car system by then or else he and his backers would lose everything. Workmen toiled down to the wire on the night of July 31 and into dawn. Finally, with Hallidie and his associates standing at the top of the Clay Street hill at Jones Street in the early-morning fog, the first cable car was ready for its test run.

Workmen pushed the car into place at the top of the hill where, according to Kahn, "the slot and tube commenced and adjusted the curiously shaped grip wheel. The grip, which was Hallidie's invention, moved up and down by means of a screw and nut on a hand wheel, and fastened its jaws securely to the cable."

The man chosen to operate the car took one look down the steep hill and bowed out, so Hallidie took the controls himself and safely "drove" the car down the hill, performing a variety of tests along the way. During this historic 2,800-foot run down a 16 percent grade, only those involved and one man looking out his window witnessed its success.

Later that day, Hallidie held a public demonstration of his horseless transportation. He noticed a few glitches in the system that he wanted to fix before putting the cable car into regular service.

At last, on September 1, 1873, the Clay Street line officially opened for business, running passengers between Kearny and Leavenworth Streets. The first cable car inspired the founding of several other cable car companies. Soon cable cars began appearing across the United States and as far away as New Zealand.

In the 1890s, San Francisco's 600 cable cars, operated by eight transit companies (which paid royalties to Hallidie), traveled 21 routes and covered 52.8 miles. By 1906, the system utilized 110 miles of track. That year, the Great San Francisco Earthquake caused extensive damage to the cable car system, resulting in a massive reduction in service.

Municipal elections in the 1940s and 1950s led the City of San Francisco to take over operation and maintenance of the cable car system. Today, MUNI (San Francisco Municipal Railway) oversees the running of the cars, which have been designated a National Historic Landmark. Though no longer a major form of transportation, San Francisco's cable cars remain a nostalgic, moving tourist attraction.

 ### To Visit: San Francisco Cable Car Museum

The City of San Francisco officially opened the cable car museum on November 10, 1967. According to its Web site, the museum "provides not only a historical perspective of the importance of the cable car to San Francisco, but an insight into the daily operations of today's system."

**San Francisco Cable Car Museum**

1201 Mason Street at Washington Street, in the Cable Car Barn and Powerhouse
San Francisco, CA 94108
415-474-1887
www.cablecarmuseum.com
Hours: April 1–September 30: daily, 10 A.M.–6 P.M.; October 1–March 31: daily, 10 A.M.–5 P.M.
Closed Thanksgiving, Christmas, and New Year's Day.
Admission free.

## WORLD'S FIRST MOTEL: THE DRIVE-BY BEDROOM

Credit for coining the term *mo-tel* (a contraction of *motor hotel*) has gone to hotelier James Vail, a Californian associated with the world's first motel.

The world's first motel was originally called the Milestone Motel and later renamed the Motel Inn. Opened on December 12, 1925, in San Luis Obispo, the historic building still stands along U.S. Route 101 but is no longer in business. *Courtesy of Teri Davis Greenberg*

The motel concept evolved from the autocamps of the 1910s and the municipal campgrounds and cottage camps of the 1920s. According to Warren J. Belasco's *Americans on the Road*, Vail visualized a chain of motor inns that would offer "antimodernist gypsies" who valued "simplicity, self-sufficiency, and comradeship" the amenities they sought as modern consumers—"comfort, service, and security."

Inspired by California's Spanish missions, situated a day's horseback ride apart, Vail, with the help of architect Arthur Heineman, planned to build 18 motor inns or "mo-tels" up the West Coast from San Diego to Seattle. Each would be a day's drive from another, and all would be designed in the Mission Revival style.

On December 12, 1925, the Milestone Motel opened for business in San Luis Obispo at 2223 Monterey Street at the foot of Cuesta Grande. It featured a red tile roof and a bell tower modeled after the Santa Barbara Mission's; 55 paneled rooms, each with an adjoining garage; and a central courtyard planted with orange, lemon, and lime trees. Gypsum board bungalows of three or four rooms backed the sturdy frame-and-stucco main building. Guests would pay $2.50 a night for the pleasure of staying at the motel.

Due to the Great Depression, Vail's dream of a string of motels never materialized. Perhaps that is why the name was eventually changed from the Milestone Motel to the Motel Inn. The motel would not be one in a chain of 18; rather, it would be one of a kind.

Today, hotelier Bob Davis owns the Motel Inn and someday plans to restore the main building. For now, however, the motel stands along U.S. Route 101 in disrepair.

---

### THE COST OF OFFERING HOSPITALITY

In the 1920s, tourist cabins cost $150 to $300 to construct, motor inns about $1,000 a unit, and large, centrally located hotels approximately $5,000 a unit. James Vail and Arthur Heineman invested more than $80,000, or nearly $1,500 a room, in the world's first motel.

---

## FIRST FREEWAY IN THE WEST: THE ARROYO SECO PARKWAY

The day before locals and tourists filled Pasadena to watch the 1941 Tournament of Roses Parade, the *Los Angeles Times* splashed this headline across its front page: "Six-Million-Dollar Arroyo Seco Parkway Opened."

Just a few months earlier, the first leg of the Pennsylvania Turnpike had opened for business. While some historians consider the turnpike to be the nation's first freeway, it was not "free." In fact, "The Dream Highway" was more a toll road than a freeway. The Arroyo Seco Parkway, though, was a true "free-way."

Constructed at a cost of $5.7 million over more than two years, the six-mile-long freeway connected downtown Los Angeles with Pasadena. President Franklin D. Roosevelt's Works Progress Administration (WPA), the Public Works Administration (PWA), the Public Roads Administration (PRA), and state and local agencies funded the Depression-era project.

December 30, 1940, brought state and federal dignitaries as well as Los Angeles officials and celebrities to the opening of the West's first nonstop roadway. Among those participating were the governor of California, California highway commissioners, the director of public works, the chief of the California Highway Patrol, and the queen of the 52nd annual Tournament of Roses Parade.

Just before Governor Culbert L. Olson and Rose Queen Sally Stanton cut the red silk-and-rose ribbon, opening the freeway to traffic for the first time, the governor delivered a prescient speech about the project:

> It takes courage to do a thing the FIRST time, no matter how simple and obvious it may appear AFTER it is done. And this, fellow citizens, is the first Freeway in the West. It is ONLY the first. And THAT is its great promise to the future—the promise of many more freeways to come.

In reality, there was and still is a major problem with the first freeway, which was renamed the Pasadena Freeway on November 18, 1954. The on- and off-ramps were (and still are) basically a right turn on or off the free-way, with stop signs and almost no merging space. *L.A. Weekly* rated the treacherous on- and off-ramps the "scariest" in the city. Fortunately,

---

### *FREEWAY DRIVING, "NERVE-FREE"?*

In December 1940, at the opening of the West's first freeway, California's governor offered this optimistic (and, in retrospect, ludicrous) prediction concerning freeway driving: "Motorists will travel over it from one end to the other in seven, eight or perhaps nine minutes . . . from the very heart of Los Angeles, through Highland Park and South Pasadena, to the very heart of Pasadena . . . in easy, nerve-free comfort and safety."

This 1940s view of the nation's first real "free-way," the Arroyo Seco Parkway, looks toward Chinatown in downtown Los Angeles. Today the roadway is known as the Pasadena Freeway. *Courtesy of the Security Pacific Collection/Los Angeles Public Library*

engineers have learned from their predecessors' mistakes. Now the area's other freeways feature long on-ramps and off-ramps that allow for safer and less nerve-racking merging into traffic.

## THE HELLS ANGELS: STARTING THEIR ENGINES IN CALIFORNIA

The first "outlaw" motorcycle gangs to catch the attention of the public comprised an eclectic array of ex-servicemen hoping to recapture the camaraderie and adventure of their World War II days and young "rebels without a cause" looking to create surrogate families.

California's exceptional climate and long stretches of asphalt gave birth to these postwar highwaymen, who first formed the Booze Fighters, the

P.O.B.O.B.'s (Pissed Off Bastards of Bloomington), and the Market Street Commandos motorcycle clubs.

On March 17, 1948, biker Otto Friedli gathered together disgruntled P.O.B.O.B.'s and other bikers on the fringe to form a motorcycle club in the San Bernardino County town of Fontana, about 50 miles east of Los Angeles. Nameless at first, the group later christened itself the Hell's Angels (the apostrophe would later be dropped). Ex–fighter pilot Arvid Olsen, who rode with Friedli and his gang (though never became a member), suggested the name from his experience as commander of the 3rd Pursuit Squadron of the Flying Tigers American Volunteer Group (AVG). One of the Flying Tigers squadrons had taken the name "Hell's Angels" from a Howard Hughes film by that name. Later, other pilots named their squadrons "Hell's Angels."

The first Hells Angels chapter shortened its name from "San Bernardino" to "Berdoo" to fit on the bottom of its jackets. For nearly six years, Berdoo was the only Hells Angels chapter. Then Stanley Kramer made *The Wild One*, starring Marlon Brando and Lee Marvin, and all hell really broke loose. This 1954 film about outlaw bikers was loosely based on a 1947 Fourth of July riot-like incident in Hollister, California, involving the P.O.B.O.B.'s and the Booze Fighters. The film spawned a cult that worshiped what Kramer depicted as America's last individualist—the rebellious, hell-bent biker.

Revved up by *The Wild One*, on August 1, 1954, San Francisco's Market Street Commandos became the second Hells Angels chapter under charter from the San Bernardino mother chapter. A year later Frank Sadliek, president of the newly formed San Francisco chapter, rode to Hollywood and bought the blue-and-yellow-striped T-shirt Lee Marvin wore in the movie. During Sadliek's 1955–62 stint as chapter president, the Hells Angels grew in notoriety.

In 1957, a 19-year-old Oakland warehouseman named Ralph Hubert "Sonny" Barger Jr. formed the third chapter of the Hells Angels. The following year, the Oakland chapter elected him president. When Berdoo's

Friedli was sent to prison in 1958, Sonny Barger took over the Hells Angels and established Oakland as the mother chapter. According to writer Yves Lavigne, Barger's vision, intelligence, and ambition transformed the Hells Angels from a "sloppy, rudderless organization into a lean, mean, no bull-shit company." The other chapters followed his lead.

Mounting police pressure in Southern California caused several Berdoo members to flee up north. Others were incarcerated, and still others had resigned from the outlaw-biker life. Thus, by the mid-1960s, Oakland had become the hub of the Hells Angels' world.

Under the informal leadership of Barger (there is no national or international president), the Hells Angels Motorcycle Club (HAMC) was incorporated in 1966, and its name and "Death's Head" insignia were later copyrighted. As media coverage of the club's raucous and often violent exploits increased, so too did its membership.

Today, with about 1,200 U.S. members and roughly 600 foreign members, the Hells Angels club is the largest organized outlaw motorcycle gang in the world. There are now HAMC chapters throughout North America, as well as in Australia, New Zealand, and South Africa, and throughout South America and Europe.

The Hells Angels motto—"Three Can Keep a Secret If Two Are Dead"—reflects the change in the organization's character since its first few years. The HAMC is no longer a bunch of raucous rebels on Harleys. Instead, law enforcement officials allege that the club has become a sophisticated organized-crime group.

## LOWRIDERS AND LOWRIDING: HOW LOW CAN YOU GO?

Los Angeles spawned the lowrider car culture during the post–World War II years. In response to white teenagers jacking up hot rods and street racing, East Los Angeles's Chicano youth began to transform their own automobiles. Instead of going for speed and muscle, however, the *pachucos* turned their cars into low, slow showpieces.

"Las Vegas," one of the lowrider vehicles featured in the "Arte y Estilo: The Lowriding Tradition" exhibit at the Petersen Automotive Museum, incorporates slot machines, champagne, and other novel, Vegas-related customized touches. *Courtesy of the Petersen Automotive Museum*

Lowriders, lowriding, and cruising may have evolved from the Mexican ritual of courting a woman by doing daring and skillful tricks astride ornately decorated horses. Decades later, cruising in lowered, customized automobiles, young Chicanos were attempting to attract women and gain the respect of their *compadres*. Soon romance took a back seat to the car itself as transforming a junked '30s or '40s Chevy into a personal and cultural statement became an expensive and time-consuming way of life that also involved car clubs, shows, and competitions.

Before the days of hydraulics, a lowrider owner would drop a car's suspension by cutting the coil springs and then placing sand-, cement-, brick-, or lead-filled bags in the trunk to lower the vehicle to within inches of the pavement. Writer Neal Becton described the early lowrider scene:

> The sight of these four-wheeled "lead-sleds" cruising down the boulevards of East L.A. became a universal symbol of Chicano culture. Painstakingly decorated with Aztec symbols, Catholic icons, street scenes and sultry Latinas, lowriders ruled the streets on hot summer nights.

When hydraulics replaced the old system of weighting down the car, they enabled lowriders to actually hop up and down and move from side to side (referred to as "car dancing").

While the typical lowrider owner spends about $800 a month on his or her car, with the finished product costing roughly $8,000 to $10,000, some enthusiasts have even been known to spend up to $70,000 on their custom creations.

Vintage 1930s to 1950s cars called "bombas" or "bombs" are usually Chevys or Fords. Most prized is the 1964 Chevrolet Impala. However, lowrider vehicles of the late 20th and early 21st centuries span almost all makes and models, including European and Japanese imports, pickup trucks, and even elaborately decorated lowrider bicycles. In fact, with about 100,000 vehicles in the United States and thousands in Europe and Japan, the lowrider phenomenon has become big business.

At the dawn of the new millennium, lowriders made their "legitimate" cultural debut in a four-month-long exhibit at the Petersen Automotive Museum called "Arte y Estilo: The Lowriding Tradition" that showcased 19 historic and highly innovative lowrider cars, trucks, and bicycles; dozens of documentary photographs featuring California lowriders; and narratives from lowrider enthusiasts such as Kita Lealao, who calls lowriders "Picassos of the boulevard."

### ☀ To Visit: Petersen Automotive Museum

Though the lowrider exhibit has moved on, car enthusiasts should not pass up a visit to the Petersen Automotive Museum.

**Petersen Automotive Museum**
6060 Wilshire Boulevard (at Fairfax Avenue)
Los Angeles, CA 90036
323-930-CARS (2277)
www.petersen.org
Hours: Tuesday-Sunday, 10 A.M.-6 P.M.
Admission charged.

## THE FOUR-LEVEL—AN INNOVATIVE INTERCHANGE

In 1944, Los Angeles engineers realized that transforming new and planned freeways into a free-flowing transportation network would require a lot of ingenuity and money. The problem concerned how to connect the Arroyo Seco Parkway, its planned southern extension (Interstate 110/the Harbor Freeway), and the Hollywood Freeway (U.S. Route 101). Lacking the necessary funds, those in charge were unable to forge ahead to find a solution.

After the state agreed to provide freeway funding, engineers began drafting plans for the freeway connection but hit a couple of bumps along the way. First, the freeway interchange was to be constructed in a densely populated area. Second, their cloverleaf-type interchange design was rejected based on its extensive space requirements and subsequent displacement of many Los Angeles residents.

Finally, in 1947, engineers unveiled plans for what would be California's first freeway-to-freeway interchange as well as the world's first four-level grade separation. A *Westways* magazine article by Matthew

Los Angeles's 47-foot-high Four-Level Interchange brings together the Hollywood, Harbor, and Pasadena Freeways. *Courtesy of the Security Pacific Collection/Los Angeles Public Library*

W. Roth described the Four-Level as an innovative interchange that would consist of "an intricate pattern of ramps that pass over and under each other on a series of bridges. . . . All vehicles transferring from one freeway to another enter and exit from the right."

Portions of the 47-foot-high interchange were completed between 1950 and 1953 with the Hollywood Freeway (the upper level) the first to be opened, followed by the Harbor Freeway and the Arroyo Seco Parkway (now known as the Pasadena Freeway) connections. Once a symbol of forward-looking Los Angeles and later a prototype for other cities, the Four-Level Interchange remains a vital link in the vast Southern California freeway system as well as an architectural icon.

## SIGALERT: TRAFFIC JAM, CALIFORNIA-STYLE

*"Sigalert: Any unplanned event that causes the closing of one lane of traffic for 30 minutes or more."*

California Highway Patrol

When radio stations broadcast a Sigalert, Southern California drivers perk up their ears, waiting to hear if they'll be delayed in arriving at work, getting home for dinner, or making an important meeting or appointment.

The Sigalert was the brainchild of Loyd C. Sigmon, an engineer at Los Angeles radio station KMPC in the 1950s and later Gene Autry's partner in Golden West Broadcasters. With the advent of television and growing competition over the airwaves, Sigmon came up with the idea of the Sigalert to draw more listeners to KMPC. He presented a proposal to the Los Angeles Police Department in which local police stations would install receivers that were activated from police headquarters, then would record officers' traffic bulletins for broadcast. The department bought the idea, and the LAPD issued the first Sigalert on Labor Day weekend of 1955.

The Sigalert's namesake, Loyd Sigmon, credits pioneer Southern California traffic reporter Bill Keene for popularizing the term. After all, Keene must have announced thousands of Sigalerts during his 37 years on the air.

Today, the California Highway Patrol administers the system using a network of computers, and all Southern California radio stations with traffic reports broadcast Sigalerts.

# "Show and Tell"
## Communications

In the 1850s, Chinese immigrants represented 10 percent of California's population. Some settled in rural areas; others clustered in Chinese ghettos. One such enclave formed in San Francisco, and in 1853, the press began referring to it as Chinatown. By the 1870s, 24 percent of California's Chinese population lived in this ethnic neighborhood they called *Dai Fou* or "Big City."

By 1880, Chinatown's population had grown to 22,000 people, densely packed into 12 blocks of wooden and brick tenements and rooming houses. They were served by numerous mercantile establishments, temples, family associations, gambling houses, and opium dens, but they lacked a fast, modern mode of communication that could accommodate various Chinese dialects.

Nearly a decade after California's first telephone exchange opened in San Francisco on February 17, 1878, Chinatown residents finally got their own. It was America's first and only such operation.

In its early years, as the Chinese Telephone Exchange's business grew, it moved from location to location. Little is known about the telephone exchange before 1906 because almost all records were destroyed in that year's massive earthquake and its ensuing fires.

Loo Kum Shu, who managed the exchange in the first decade of the 20th century, explained the telephone's importance to Chinatown's residents:

> The telephone is an important factor of life in Chinatown. The Chinese use it a great deal and often transact very important business over the wire. For this reason we have no party wires, but each number has its own wire. If this were not the case we could not get any of the Chinese to use the phones under any circumstances. As it is, however, they use them all the time. . . . We are going to put in at least 150 phones during the coming year [1909], so you see we are prospering greatly.

Under Loo Kum Shu's management, all of the operators were Chinese men, though the manager would have preferred to hire female operators "for many reasons, chiefly on account of good temper." Because the

The Chinese Telephone Exchange moved from location to location as it grew before settling into this "Chinese-style" building in 1909. San Francisco's Pacific Telephone Chinese exchange was the only Chinese-language telephone exchange outside China. *Courtesy of Teri Davis Greenberg*

women would have had to be "purchased outright" and guarded, and a chaperone hired "to look after the proprieties," the cost of employing women would have been prohibitive.

One observer of the exchange in 1909 noted that the Chinese operators had the almost impossible task of memorizing the names and addresses of nearly 1,500 subscribers. There were 255 numbers on the exchange, and 125 more telephones in clubs and rooming houses. When callers dialed up the exchange, they never gave a phone number; instead, they asked for a person by name. The operator had to immediately remember the number of the person requested and connect the caller with him or her. The observer said that the operators seemed to perform their work "without effort."

The manager made the job his life. When the new building for the exchange was constructed in 1909, it included a bedroom, dining room, and small kitchen for the manager, who actually lived on-site. In fact, he was on call 24 hours a day, 365 days a year.

By the 1920s, the exchange was called the "China 5" because during the day a Chinese woman and her California-born daughters, who were all fluent in five Chinese dialects, staffed the switchboard. (Male operators worked the night shift.) Because of their connections with nearly everyone in the city and their "tenacious memories," these women happened to know where their subscribers could most likely be reached when not at home.

The Chinese telephone exchange lasted until 1949, when the direct-dial telephone system became commonplace. Just before it shut down, the exchange employed 20 operators, all fluent in five Chinese dialects and all with amazing memories. Its closing signaled the end of an era in Bay Area history.

## A San Francisco Architectural First

While San Francisco's city fathers were deciding where to relocate the Chinese population after the 1906 earthquake's fires destroyed Chinatown, an American-born Chinese businessman named Look Tin Eli took out a $3 million loan from Hong Kong and rebuilt Chinatown on its original site.

Unlike the original neighborhood of mostly Italianate buildings, Look planned to give the area an "Oriental" appearance to draw non-Chinese San Franciscans and visiting tourists. Unable to find any local Chinese architects, Look hired Caucasian ones who ended up designing their version of a Chinese neighborhood that looked like "a stage-set China."

The three-tiered, three-story Chinese Telephone Exchange building, completed in 1909, was the first example of Chinese-style architecture in San Francisco. The first floor was occupied by a store, with the telephone exchange at the top of a long flight of stairs.

While the Chinese Telephone Exchange no longer exists, the historic building still stands at 743 Washington Street, between Kearny Street and Grant Avenue. It houses the Chinatown branch of the Bank of Canton of California.

## ELECTRONIC TELEVISION: A SAN FRANCISCO PREMIERE

Philo T. Farnsworth began creating his "television system" in a one-bedroom Hollywood apartment and continued his research and development in a second-story loft in San Francisco. Located at 202 Green Street, Farnsworth's San Francisco lab is considered both the birthplace of electronic television and the site of its first successful laboratory demonstration. (The first public demonstration took place in Philadelphia in 1934.)

The self-taught electrical engineer conceived the idea for electronic television as a teenager mowing hay on the family farm. He visualized the horizontal rows of hay as lines on a television screen. Having previously read about mechanical television in science books and *Popular Science,* he believed there had to be a way to remove the moving parts from television to provide better reception. In 1922, the 16-year-old sketched a diagram of his electronic-television idea for his science teacher, Justin Tolman.

Farnsworth attended Brigham Young University but had to drop out for financial reasons after his father died. In Salt Lake City he met a professional fund-raiser from Los Angeles named George Everson, who hired him to help run a Community Chest campaign. One day the younger man told Everson about his idea for a television system and lamented his lack of funds to finance the project. Intrigued with the idea, Everson invested $6,000 but insisted that Farnsworth move to the Los Angeles area to be closer to big-city resources. So the young inventor and his new bride, Elma, nicknamed Pem, packed up and moved to Hollywood.

Once established in an apartment, Farnsworth quickly set up a workshop in his dining room. He had to create from scratch many of the parts and tools he needed, which entailed learning electrochemistry, radio electronics, and glassblowing as well as scavenging the city for raw materials. Odd-looking objects and materials filled the small apartment and raised suspicion among neighbors. Because it was the Prohibition era, the young couple were suspected of building a still. Neighbors reported them to the police, who subsequently searched the apartment and questioned the Farnsworths. Philo told them he was building a television system. Unfamiliar with "television," the bewildered police left the apartment.

George Everson realized that $6,000 was inadequate to finance Farnsworth's project and that he would need more backers. Before he would ask anyone else to invest in the project, however, he solicited the opinion of Professor Mott Smith of the California Institute of Technology.

Philo Farnsworth, the creator of electronic television, posed for this photo showing the 1929 version of his "continuous television transmitter." *Courtesy of the J. Willard Marriott Library, Manuscripts Division, University of Utah*

After a four-hour talk with Farnsworth, Smith pronounced the invention possible and Farnsworth capable of creating it.

Confident that he could secure bank funding for Farnsworth's television, Everson traveled to San Francisco in August 1926 to meet with Crocker Bank officials. Soon after, the bankers, known as the Crocker Group, requested Farnsworth's presence. After meeting with Farnsworth, Crocker agreed to put up $25,000 toward the television project, but the bankers wanted the inventor to move to San Francisco to continue his work. They offered the use of half of the second floor of a Green Street building for a laboratory.

Once again, the Farnsworths found themselves packing and moving. Pem and Philo invited Pem's brother Cliff Gardner to join them in San

Francisco. He came. Farnsworth's brother-in-law found himself chief glassblower, even though he had no previous experience in the craft. Using his newly acquired glassblowing skills, Gardner fashioned the first electronic television camera tube—Farnsworth's Image Dissector—to transmit images. For an image receiver, Farnsworth used a standard chemical flask that he named an Image Oscillite.

On January 7, 1927, Farnsworth submitted his application for his first patent for the electronic television system. This date is traditionally considered the birth of the television as we know it.

In late summer 1927, Farnsworth and Gardner put together the first television device and began testing it. With each failure to send an image to the receiver, Farnsworth went back to the drawing board. When he was satisfied the television was ready for a demonstration, he invited George Everson and Pem to watch the first transmission.

Farnsworth decided to transmit the image of a simple, thick straight line because it could be rotated vertically and horizontally. With Gardner in one room and Farnsworth and the others in another, Gardner began the transmission that would change the world of communications forever. The demonstration was a success. As Everson put it in a telegram to partner Les Gorrell in Los Angeles: "The damned thing works!"

Farnsworth and his "lab gang," as he called his employees, worked on perfecting the "continuous television transmitter" for the rest of that year and into the spring of 1928. Farnsworth's goal was to improve image clarity by increasing the number of scan lines from about 60 lines per frame to 400. (In comparison, mechanical television could scan 50 lines per frame, a blurred mess at best.)

Because of the tremendous amount of money the Crocker Group officials had invested in Farnsworth's television, they prodded Farnsworth into setting up a demonstration for them. Thus, in May 1928, the second demonstration of electronic television took place at the Green Street lab. Nobody in the audience had ever seen a television before. This time, to appeal to the bankers, Farnsworth decided to transmit the image of a dollar sign. When the image materialized before the bankers' eyes, they were amazed. They also foresaw the dollar signs to be made from television if they were to sell it to a big electrical company.

Farnsworth did not want to sell the invention outright; he wanted to retain all patents on the television and subsequent improvements to it and then license the rights. Everson managed to get the bankers to table the motion to sell.

Not long after the following front-page headline ran in the September 3, 1928, *San Francisco Chronicle*—"SF MAN'S INVENTION TO REVOLU-TIONIZE TELEVISION"—a fire broke out in the Green Street lab, destroying Farnsworth's equipment. The lab gang, now in a mad rush to make their television commercially salable, immediately went to work to rebuild. Then, in 1929, the Crocker Group ceased funding the project.

Farnsworth was forced to lay off some of his staff but promised to rehire them as soon as he could. When Jess McCargar, formerly with Crocker Bank, and George Everson bought out the rest of the Crocker Group, they reincorporated as Television Laboratories. In May 1929, they renamed the company Farnsworth Television, Inc., of California.

Meanwhile, on the East Coast, RCA head David Sarnoff heard about Farnsworth's invention and sent Vladimir Zworykin to visit Farnsworth's lab to "check out" the television. Research engineer Zworykin had also developed and patented a television system, but it was different from Farnsworth's. Seeing what Farnsworth had done helped him perfect his own system. After Zworykin reported what he had seen, Sarnoff paid a visit to Farnsworth, watched a television demonstration, talked to Farnsworth about his invention, and then offered to buy the company from Everson for $100,000 if Farnsworth came with it. Everson turned him down.

In 1931, Philco Radio Corporation of Philadelphia became the company's first licensee and offered to foot the bill for Farnsworth's ongoing research if he agreed to relocate the company to Philadelphia to help Philco get into the television business. Pem didn't want to leave their new San Francisco home, but Farnsworth assured her that the move would be only temporary and that they would return to San Francisco in the fall. At the time, the East Coast was the hub of the electronics industry. The Farnsworths didn't return to San Francisco.

The years that followed were filled with frustration for Farnsworth after RCA introduced its own version of electronic television. Farnsworth found himself entangled in patent wars with the giant company. After years of litigation, he emerged victorious over RCA. As a result, the corporation was forced to pay royalties to Farnsworth. It marked the first time in RCA's history that it was a patent licensee, not a patent holder.

## DISNEY ANIMATED FILMS: EMPIRE OF FIRSTS

Today's Walt Disney Company and animators the world over owe much of their success to Walter Elias Disney, who started it all when he stepped off a train in Los Angeles in 1923 and founded Disney Brothers Studio in Hollywood with his brother Roy. (Walt later relocated the studio to Burbank.)

From the imagination and determination of Walt Disney developed a string of animation firsts that have had a tremendous impact on the entertainment industry. *Steamboat Willie*, a series called "Silly Symphonies," *Snow White and the Seven Dwarfs*, and, years after Walt's death, *Toy Story* all advanced the art of animation.

*Steamboat Willie*, released on November 18, 1928, introduced the character of Mickey Mouse, and its release date is considered Mickey's "official" birthday. Walt created Mickey on a train trip from New York to Los Angeles after another character he had created—Oswald the Lucky Rabbit—was virtually stolen from him by his film distributor.

Technically, *Steamboat Willie* was the first cartoon to successfully incorporate synchronized sound. Walt contracted with a man named Pat Powers who used what he called Cinephone to carry out the difficult process of synchronizing the sound and animation. After initial recording sessions failed to produce a satisfactory result, Walt recorded the soundtrack with a 15-piece orchestra and supplied Mickey's voice himself.

WALT DISNEY'S

MICKEY MOUSE

iN

STEAMBOAT WILLIE

Mickey Mouse made his film debut in *Steamboat Willie,* the first cartoon to successfully incorporate synchronized sound. ©*Disney Enterprises, Inc.*

Powers distributed the cartoon, which proved a hit with both critics and the public, and Mickey went on to symbolize the Disney empire.

Inspired by an idea from songwriter Carl Stalling, Walt then decided to produce a series of animated shorts in which the visuals would take a back seat to the music. Called "Silly Symphonies," these cartoons gave Disney animators the freedom to experiment. Set to popular and classical music, and sometimes avant-garde, these cartoons broke the animation mold of the time with their lack of plot lines and no recurring characters. Walt assigned a group of animators separate from the Mickey Mouse artists to work on them. Disney's 29th Silly Symphony, *Flowers and Trees*, was the first to be rendered entirely in Technicolor. It won an Academy Award in 1932. *The Old Mill* (1937) was the first animated film to achieve a three-dimensional look through the use of the "multiplane" camera, which soon became standard in animation studios. Disney's animators created 75 Silly Symphonies from 1929 to 1939.

With a running time of 83 minutes, *Snow White and the Seven Dwarfs* holds the distinction of being the world's first full-length animated feature film. It took three years and 750 animators to produce and gave us such classic songs as "Someday My Prince Will Come," "Heigh Ho," and "Whistle While You Work." When Walt first brought up the possibility of a full-length cartoon, critics referred to the project as Disney's Folly. Yet, following the film's premiere at the Carthay Circle Theater in Los Angeles on December 21, 1937, Walt proved his critics wrong. The film struck a chord with adults as well as with children and proved a big commercial success.

Walt Disney's *Snow White and the Seven Dwarfs,* the world's first full-length animated film, delighted both children and adults when it debuted in Los Angeles in 1937.
© *Disney Enterprises, Inc.*

It cost Disney $1.4 million to produce, and in its original release *Snow White and the Seven Dwarfs* grossed $8.5 million (at 10 cents a ticket!). At the 1939 Academy Awards, Shirley Temple presented Walt with a special Academy Award for the film, consisting of one regular-size Oscar statuette and seven smaller ones.

Walt followed up *Snow White and the Seven Dwarfs* with a number of other animated features produced under his direction: *Pinocchio* (1940), *Fantasia* (1940), *Dumbo* (1941), *Bambi* (1942), *Alice in Wonderland* (1951), *Peter Pan* (1953), *Lady and the Tramp* (1955), *Sleeping Beauty* (1959), *101 Dalmatians* (1961), *The Sword in the Stone* (1963), *Winnie the Pooh and the Honey Tree* (1966; a 26-minute "featurette"), and *The Jungle Book* (1967).

Though Walt Disney passed away from lung cancer in 1966, he left a legacy of imagination and innovation for subsequent Disney animators and filmmakers to build upon. *Toy Story* (1995) represents still another animation first for Disney as well as a first for Northern California–based Pixar Animation Studios. The collaborative venture produced the first entirely computer-generated animated feature film. The Academy of Motion Picture Arts and Sciences recognized *Toy Story* director John Lasseter "for the development and inspired application of techniques

---

### FIRST MOTION PICTURE TO MAKE
### EXTENSIVE USE OF COMPUTER IMAGERY

In July 1982, the Walt Disney Company released *Tron,* a live-action film starring Jeff Bridges and Bruce Boxleitner. *Star Wars* and *West World* had already used computer imagery to generate special effects, but *Tron's* filmmakers, in conjunction with two Los Angeles and two New York computer and special effects firms, used computers to create an entire three-dimensional world. The film was shot on sound stages at Disney Studios in Burbank, on location in Los Angeles, and at Lawrence Livermore Laboratory outside Oakland.

that have made possible the first feature-length computer-animated film." If the past can be used to predict the future, more Disney firsts are on the horizon.

## SPREAD SPECTRUM TECHNOLOGY: A MOVIE STAR, A COMPOSER, AND A BRAINSTORM

In the early 1940s, movie star Hedy Lamarr and avant-garde composer George Antheil invented and patented the concept of frequency hopping, a form of today's spread spectrum technology. With the advent of the microprocessor, Lamarr and Antheil's prescient idea has been incorporated into U.S. Department of Defense satellite systems as well as into wireless Internet connections and cellular and cordless phones.

Lamarr, MGM's "most beautiful girl in the world," and Antheil, known as "the bad boy of music," seem an unlikely pair of inventors. Yet a look into their pasts reveals two intellectually gifted people who happened to be performing artists. One was informally schooled in the workings of World War II–era munitions and the other in "thinking outside the box."

Born Hedwig Eva Maria Kiesler in Vienna about 1914, Hedy Lamarr was forced into an arranged marriage with wealthy armaments manufacturer Fritz Mandl. By all accounts, Mandl was a controlling man who forced his 19-year-old bride to accompany him to business dinners with guests who included Mussolini and, possibly, Hitler. While entertaining her husband's business associates, the intelligent young beauty was also learning about Nazi plans for the use of munitions. Mandl unwittingly furthered Lamarr's education in how to defeat the Nazis (for whom she harbored a secret, intense hatred) when he forced her to join him in watching field-test films on torpedo systems.

When she could no longer tolerate her home situation, Lamarr decided to escape from Mandl. After an initial unsuccessful attempt, she managed to get away by drugging the maid guarding her. She escaped to London and shortly thereafter began appearing on the British stage. Louis B. Mayer discovered the beauty and signed her to a contract with

MGM but insisted that Hedy Kiesler change her surname. So she became Hedy Lamarr.

Meanwhile, George Antheil's story coincides with the 1920s Paris expatriate scene. Friendly with Ezra Pound and other famous writers, artists, and musicians experimenting with new forms of art and thought, Antheil became part of the modern art movement. One of his modernist musical compositions, "Ballet Mechanique," represented one of the first examples of a musical piece scored with the use of machines. The musical breakthrough featured 14 player pianos simultaneously playing in synchronization. Antheil's ability to synchronize the pianos helped inspire the invention of frequency hopping.

After Lamarr met Antheil at a dinner party hosted by Janet Gaynor, Lamarr scrawled her phone number in lipstick on the windshield of his

Hedy Lamarr looks anything but the inventor of spread spectrum technology in this sexy 1946 photo. Then again, she *was* the first woman to appear nude in a major film. *Courtesy of AP/Worldwide Photos*

car. He called, and the two soon met at Lamarr's Benedict Canyon home. While Antheil sat at the piano playing a series of notes, Lamarr followed along on the keyboard. Suddenly she blurted out, "Hey, look, we're talking to each other and we're changing all the time." This simple statement-turned-epiphany led Lamarr to equate the changing note patterns on the piano with a similar system for radio signals that could be employed in torpedo guidance and signal scrambling. The next day, she and Antheil met to work out such a system.

According to Associated Press cyberspace writer Elizabeth Weise, Lamarr reasoned:

> A simple radio signal sent to control a torpedo was too easy to block. But what if the signal hopped from frequency to frequency at split-second intervals? Anyone trying to listen in or jam it would hear only random noise, like a radio dial being spun. But if both the sender and the receiver were hopping in synch, the message would come through loud and clear.

While the initial concept was Lamarr's, Antheil contributed the idea of using piano rolls to ensure synchronization of sender and receiver.

After months of concentrated thought and effort on the project, the two finally filed an application to patent their "Secret Communication System" on June 10, 1941. Fourteen months later, on August 11, 1942, "Hedy Kiesler Markey, Los Angeles, and George Antheil, Manhattan Beach, Calif." were granted U.S. Patent 2,292,387.

The idea was way ahead of its time, and the U.S. Navy considered it too cumbersome for the war effort. Not until the invention of the transistor in the late 1940s did the military see the practical application of the Lamarr/Antheil system. Three years after the patent lapsed, the technology was finally employed on U.S. ships involved in the 1962 Cuban missile crisis.

The introduction of Intel's 4004 microprocessor in 1971 helped to make spread spectrum technology even more efficient and cost-effective and signaled the beginning of its widespread use in military and commercial applications that continues into the 21st century. Though all of these new and future developments are and will be based on Lamarr and Antheil's 1940s "Secret Communication System," sadly, neither inventor ever received a penny in royalties due to the expiration of the 17-year patent period.

## Long-Overdue Recognition

On March 12, 1997, at the Computers, Freedom, and Privacy conference in Burlingame, Lamarr and Antheil were honored with the Pioneer Award of the Electronic Frequency Foundation (EFF) for their contribution to society through their seminal invention of frequency-hopping technology.

Mike Godwin, a member of the Pioneer Awards' panel of judges and coordinator of the awards event, said that the EFF considers "both Lamarr's contribution and the general public's 'nearly absolute ignorance about it' to merit special recognition for Lamarr as well as for the late George Antheil, who, working with Lamarr more than half a century ago, developed and patented what is now known as spread-spectrum [*sic*] broadcasting."

Though Antheil died in 1959 and Lamarr was unable to attend the awards ceremony, the executor of Antheil's estate and Lamarr's son, Anthony Loder, accepted the award on their behalf. Hedy Lamarr passed away on January 18, 2000.

Would you believe the Internet owes its existence to the Cold War and the threat of nuclear attack? Yes, it's true. So the next time you log on to the Internet, pay homage to the U.S. Department of Defense, the U.S. taxpayer, and the University of California.

In 1958, in response to the Soviet Union's launch of *Sputnik*, President Dwight D. Eisenhower created the Advanced Research Projects Agency (ARPA) within the Department of Defense to develop America's first successful satellite. Within 18 months, U.S. scientists had developed *Explorer I*, and the space race had begun.

Due to the perceived threat of Soviet nuclear attack, the Cold War forced the Defense Department to redirect ARPA's efforts to the development of a computer-based network communications system. In 1962, Dr. J. C. R. "Lick" Licklider was appointed head of ARPA and directed to develop a system of interactive computers located in dispersed locations. Not establishing a centralized information headquarters target meant that even if one computer on the network were destroyed or incapacitated by enemy attack, the others could still communicate with each other.

A couple of years later, Leonard Kleinrock's book *Communication Nets* introduced "packet switching," the technology that made the Internet possible. In 1963, Kleinrock joined the faculty of the University of California, Los Angeles (UCLA) as an expert in computer networking, and soon ARPA asked him to play a major role in developing what would become the ARPANET. Due largely to Kleinrock's association with UCLA, ARPA chose the university to be the first node on the ARPANET. (Three other node locations were also selected: the Stanford Research Institute [SRI], the University of California at Santa Barbara, and the University of Utah.)

On September 1, 1969, ARPA linked its first switch, or Information Message Processor (IMP), to UCLA's computer. Everyone with any connection to the project—from representatives of the local telephone company and the companies that had manufactured the IMP minicomputer and the UCLA host computer to UCLA campus administration and the computer science department's administration—showed up for the demonstration of the new technology. As testament to Kleinrock and his team's phenomenal job (and to their relief), the demonstration proved successful as bits of information moved between the UCLA computer and the IMP. Within a day, messages were moving between the computers. The ARPANET, grandfather of the Internet, had been born in Los Angeles.

A month later, the first host-to-host message was sent from UCLA to SRI. Attempting to type *logon* and send the message to Palo Alto, the UCLA programmer typed *l* and asked the Stanford programmers if they had received it. The answer via telephone headset was "Got the *l*." Next, UCLA sent *o* and received the answer "Got the *o*." Then, when UCLA typed in the *g*, the system crashed! Determined to make the system work, Kleinrock and his programmer tried again and were successful.

In 1983, because so many people had access to the ARPANET, the network was split into the ARPANET and MILNET (the Defense Data Network) for national security reasons. In 1986, the National Science Foundation formed a new, competing computer network named NSFNET, which every major university soon joined. Using a faster Internet Protocol (IP) software than the ARPANET, this new network soon replaced its predecessor and formed the system today referred to as the Internet. The ARPANET came to an end in 1990.

# "Weird Science"
## Science and Technology

### THE RICHTER SCALE: "I GIVE THAT QUAKE A 6.8"

Living in California has its ups and downs—literally. Hundreds of earthquakes occur daily, but most are imperceptible to humans. Occasionally, though, large quakes strike, taking lives, causing injuries, destroying property, and reminding us that Mother Nature can throw a knock-out punch we didn't see coming.

For more than a hundred years, scientists have been measuring earthquakes. The first quake-measuring systems, the Forel-Rossi scale and the Mercali scale, were highly subjective. In 1931, scientists at the Pasadena-based Seismological Laboratory of the Carnegie Institution of Washington, D.C., began using the modified Mercali scale to assess earthquake intensity based on the damage done. Taken into account were the "type and strength of substrate materials, the distance from the epicenter, the magnitude of the quake, the type of building structure, and the duration of the shaking."

In the mid-1930s, also at the Seismological Laboratory, physicist Charles Richter of the California Institute of Technology (Caltech) and a colleague, geophysicist/mathematician Beno Gutenberg, developed a more accurate, objective way to measure quakes. (For reasons unknown, though both Richter and Gutenberg invented the earthquake magnitude scale, it became known as the Richter scale and not the Gutenberg-Richter scale.)

Richter, who pursued his higher education at the University of Southern California, Stanford University, and Caltech, began working at the Seismological Laboratory in 1927. The following year, he received his doctorate in theoretical physics from Caltech. Between 1936 and 1970, Richter served as a professor of seismology at the university.

Gutenberg, a German immigrant known as "the foremost observational seismologist of the twentieth century," first visited the Seismological Laboratory in 1929, and when offered a position there in 1930, accepted it, along with a professorship in geophysics at Caltech.

In 1936, the Seismological Laboratory became part of Caltech under the direction of H. O. Wood, one of the developers of the modified Mercali scale. In 1935, when Wood fell ill, Gutenberg became de facto director of the lab. Upon Wood's retirement in 1947, Gutenberg officially replaced him as lab director.

In the mid-to-late 1930s, Gutenberg and Richter cowrote a series of papers titled *On Seismic Waves* that established the foundation for modern observational seismology. After studying seismographic data on the 200-plus Southern California earthquakes that occurred annually, Richter began thinking about a more objective and quantitative way to measure quakes than using the modified Mercali scale. In his own words:

> In the course of historical or statistical study of earthquakes in any given region it is frequently desirable to have a scale for rating these shocks in terms of their original energy, independently of the effects which may be produced at any particular point of observation.

In 1935, with input from Gutenberg, Richter formulated a "local magnitude scale" for determining the size of Southern California earthquakes. The following year, Gutenberg and Richter constructed a "surface wave magnitude scale" for distant earthquakes. This second scale made possible, for the first time, the accurate measurement of great earthquakes.

When quake vibrations (seismic waves) travel through the earth, they are recorded on an instrument called a seismograph. With the logarithmic Richter scale, scientists can approximate energy released by a quake using an equation that includes magnitude and distance from the seismograph to the epicenter of the earthquake.

On the Richter scale, quake magnitude is expressed in whole numbers (0 to 9) and decimal fractions, with each successive whole number representing an increase in magnitude 10 times that represented by the whole number before it. In addition, each whole-number step in magnitude represents the release of about 31 times more energy than the preceding whole-number value.

The Richter scale's drawback is that it really can't be used to express quake damage. For example, in the case of two major earthquakes of the exact same magnitude, one occurring in a populated, urban area and the other in a remote area, the former may cause death, injury, and property destruction, while the latter will result in no damage.

## Numbers on the Scale

A magnitude 1 earthquake can be detected only by instruments; a magnitude 2 (10 times a number 1 quake), only by "sensitive people" and animals; a 3 (100 times a number 1 quake) will be felt by many people and can be compared with what it feels like when an 18-wheeler rumbles by; a 4 (1,000 times a number 1) will be felt by almost everyone, and some pictures may fall off walls and items may topple from shelves; a magnitude 5 quake (10,000 times a number 1) may cause some weak walls to crack and even fall down; a 6 (100,000 times a number 1) is destructive and will cause considerable damage in populated areas; a magnitude 7 earthquake (1 million times a number 1) will result in serious and widespread damage; and an 8 (10 million times a number 1) will cause massive destruction not only near the epicenter but also in surrounding communities.

## THE RUBY LASER: A LIGHT WAVE FROM MALIBU

In 1960, physicist and electrical engineer Theodore "Ted" Maiman, a Los Angeles native, invented the first operable laser while employed at Hughes Research Laboratory (HRL) in Malibu. A laser, an acronym for "light amplification by stimulated emission of radiation," creates, amplifies, and transmits a narrow beam of intensely focused (coherent) light.

Maiman's work on the Ruby Laser System, its patented name, was an outgrowth of his doctoral research at Stanford University and his reading of a classic article titled "Infrared and Optical Masers." The article provided a general description of how to build a laser as well as a list of problems involved in its creation. Immediately after the article's publication, scientists around the globe rushed to be first to produce a working laser.

In a 1984 interview, Maiman talked about his entrance into the "laser race": "There it was, August 1959, and I was aware of the fact that people all over the world were now in this race. It was a little brash for me to enter that race at that time. People with well-funded efforts had already been doing [research] for, let's say, a year."

In 1998, the American public voted for the laser as a symbol of the 1960s worthy of its own postage stamp in the U.S. Postal Service's "Celebrate the Century—1960s" contest. Ted Maiman invented the first laser at Hughes Research Laboratory in Malibu in 1960.

While other scientists were debating the merits of various materials to use in the laser, Maiman forged ahead with a synthetic ruby despite its rejection by the scientific community. Until Maiman verified with crystal experts that the ruby was, indeed, a suitable laser material, the ruby was thought by all to have only a 1 percent chance of working. Even his bosses at HRL doubted the ruby would work. In fact, at the time he first demonstrated the ruby laser on May 16, 1960, his project had virtually been canceled.

What makes Maiman's accomplishment even more remarkable is the discrepancy between HRL's and other labs' laser-research budgets ($50,000 versus $500,000 to $1 million). Furthermore, not only did Maiman win the laser race, but he also crossed the finish line in a mere nine months.

Laser research and development continued after the introduction of Maiman's pink ruby solid-state, high-intensity laser. (Solid-state lasers emit the highest output power of all lasers.) Gas, liquid, and semiconductor lasers followed and found applications in the fields of medicine, surgery, industry, communications, and scientific research.

For HRL, Maiman's ruby laser "became the cornerstone of a multibillion-dollar laser range finder business" and sparked a long list of successful projects in research and development.

## THE COMPUTER MOUSE: POINT-AND-CLICK TOOL FOR THOUGHT

*"The mouse was the first revolutionary step [toward] making computers interact directly with human beings."*

Paul Saffo, president, Institute for the Future

Each time someone uses a personal computer, he or she most probably works with one or more concepts or products created by Douglas C. Engelbart. Though the Northern California resident has patented more than two dozen computer-related inventions, perhaps his most famous is the "X-Y Position Indicator for a Display System," better known as the computer "mouse."

As a World War II Navy electronics and radar technician, Engelbart became interested in computers in 1945 after reading an article about technology in *The Atlantic Monthly* written by Vannevar Bush, the highest-ranking scientific administrator in the U.S. war effort.

Five years later, inspired by Bush's ideas, newly graduated electrical engineer Engelbart began contemplating the notion of augmenting human intelligence through machines. In Engelbart's own words:

> When I first heard about computers, I understood, from my radar experience, that if these machines can show you information on punchcards and printouts on paper, they could write or draw that information on a screen. When I saw the connection between a cathode-ray screen, an information processor, and a medium for representing symbols to a person, it all tumbled together in about half an hour.

Engelbart's first engineering position was with the Ames Laboratory of the National Advisory Committee for Aeronautics, on the San Francisco peninsula. In 1951, he left Ames to attend graduate school at the University of California at Berkeley. After earning his Ph.D. in 1955, Engelbart remained on campus as an acting assistant professor. When one of his colleagues warned him that his "wild ideas" would stunt his professional growth in academia, Engelbart left the university and accepted a job at the Stanford Research Institute (SRI) in Menlo Park.

In 1963, while at SRI, Engelbart was granted the funds to start his own research lab, later called the Augmentation Research Center (ARC). Staffed by William K. English, Jeff Rulifson, and Engelbart, ARC pioneered an innovative and sophisticated system called oNLine System, or NLS. Before certain key features of the revolutionary NLS (later called "hypertext") could be created, however, Engelbart and his SRI/ARC team had to develop a special set of "tools"—one of which was the "mouse."

As Engelbart tells it, the idea for the mouse came from "five minutes of invention while sitting at a conference." The mouse minimizes the use of the computer keyboard as a means of manipulating data. The electro-mechanical device senses movement in both X and Y directions and then relays that information to the computer. The computer software, based on the X-Y information, generates the cursor's shape and size and positions the cursor on the screen. (The positioning on the screen is a relative position, not the absolute position of the mouse itself.) The mouse also contains one to three switches that, when activated by pushing a button, cause the computer to perform a function related to the cursor's position.

By 1968, ARC had grown to 17 people, the staff had updated its computer system three times, and its early experimental software had evolved into what writer Howard Rheingold refers to as a "real working tool kit for information specialists." Engelbart decided it was time to share the center's work with the rest of the computer community.

On December 9, 1968, at the Fall Joint Computer Conference, Engelbart and his team presented a spectacular demonstration that wowed even the most avid computer aficionados. A curious and, at first, skeptical audience sat in San Francisco's Civic Auditorium watching Engelbart and SRI/ARC staff members (the latter located 25 miles away and equipped with a 192 kb mainframe computer) jointly present a multimedia demonstration of a mouse-driven, Windows-like graphical user interface via shared-screen teleconferencing. The crowd was awed and showed its reverence for Engelbart by giving him a standing ovation. Years later, Andy van Dam, the Thomas J. Watson, Jr., University Professor of Technology and Education at Brown University, dubbed the presentation "The Mother of All Demos."

At its 1968 debut, the computer mouse (so called because "the tail came out") was a nondescript, two-wheeled metal box built by Bill English to his boss's specifications. It functioned as Engelbart's "magic wand" during the 90-minute demonstration of key features of the NLS: outline editors, hypertext linking, word processing, e-mail, and user configurability and programmability. Without the mouse, none of these innovations would have been feasible.

Engelbart originally received only $10,000 for the mouse, but in April 1997 he was awarded the Lemelson-MIT Prize and $500,000. At the award ceremony, Engelbart was recognized for his achievement in inventing "the interface between computers and human beings."

## THE MICROPROCESSOR: INTEL'S COMPUTER ON A CHIP

*"When I first started working with computers, they were under the control of managers who decided who would have access and what types of usage would be allowed. My greatest satisfaction has come from seeing the microprocessor take control away from those despots and make computing power available to everyone."*

Ted Hoff, microprocessor inventor

Between 1969 and 1971, Ted Hoff, Stan Mazor, and Federico Faggin of Intel and Masatoshi Shima of Busicom, a Japanese firm, developed and built the world's first microprocessor in Santa Clara. This "computer on a chip" proved to be, as Intel cofounder Gordon Moore stated, "one of the most revolutionary products in the history of mankind."

Busicom had approached Intel (short for "integrated electronics") in April 1969 to complete the design and manufacture of a set of silicon chips for a new calculator. Busicom's original design called for 12 separate chips to handle keyboard scanning, display control, printer control, and other functions. Stanford-educated Dr. Marcian Edward "Ted" Hoff Jr., who had begun working at Intel in 1962 as manager of applications research, was assigned the calculator project. Not pleased that the Japanese design would result in a calculator that would cost as much as a minicomputer, Hoff came up with an alternative architecture, or design. Hoff's architecture for a general-purpose computer central processing unit (CPU) consisting of a single silicon chip would be considerably cheaper to mass-produce and, unlike the fixed-program Japanese design, could be reprogrammed to perform different functions. This innovation meant the microprocessor could act like any kind of calculator Busicom wanted.

After a series of meetings with Busicom representatives, Intel was given the go-ahead to use Hoff's single-chip architecture. Hoff was subsequently recognized as the first person to launch and actually execute a microprocessor project, leading the *Economist* to call him "one of the seven most influential scientists since World War II." Though Hoff envisioned the architecture for the first microprocessor, and is often credited as the sole inventor, he was actually part of a team of engineers that brought the chip to fruition.

Stanley Mazor joined Intel and Hoff's team in September 1969. Having studied mathematics and computer programming at San Francisco State University and worked as a programmer and computer designer at Fairchild Semiconductor in Palo Alto, Mazor was well qualified for the Busicom project. He helped Hoff solve a number of design problems involving the microprocessor's architecture.

Then, in April 1970, engineer Federico Faggin, originally from Italy, left his position at Fairchild, came on board at Intel, and joined the Busicom project team. Faggin had developed the original silicon gate technology for transistor design while working for Fairchild; at Intel, he was responsible for writing the software for the new chip. With help from Mazor and Busicom's Masatoshi Shima, Faggin produced the completed microprocessor from Hoff's original architecture.

In February 1971 the Intel team delivered the first working microprocessor to Busicom, but, recognizing the product's potential, Intel bought back the rights to the microprocessor from the Japanese company. About nine months later, Intel formally announced its 4004 CPU (microprocessor) in *Electronic News*, heralding "a new era of integrated electronics" with the company's "microprogrammable computer on a chip."

Intel designated the first microprocessor the 4004 based on the approximate number of transistors that the single chip replaced. The 4004 contained 2,300 transistors etched into the silicon. It ran at 108 kilohertz, measured one-eighth of an inch by one-sixteenth of an inch, and could perform nearly any computation. The tiny 4004 was as powerful as the first mainframe computer, the ENIAC, which utilized 18,000 vacuum tubes and occupied 3,000 cubic feet of space. And the first microprocessor cost less to buy in 1971 than an IBM 1620 computer from the early 1960s cost to lease for one day!

The invention of the microprocessor also meant that programming intelligence into inanimate objects was now possible. The first microprocessor even entered the Asteroid Belt aboard the *Pioneer 10* in 1972. Today, nearly all computers, medical devices, and automobiles, not to mention microwave ovens, telephone speed-dial and redial features, automatic thermostats, and other common devices, utilize microprocessor technology.

### ☀ *To Visit: The Intel Museum*

To learn about the history of the microprocessor, about how computer chips are made and how transistors and microprocessors work, or about "clean rooms" and memory technology, visit the Intel Museum. Tours are available if scheduled in advance.

**The Intel Museum**
Intel Corporation's Robert Noyce Building
Main Lobby
2200 Mission College Boulevard
Santa Clara, CA 95052-8119
408-765-0503
Hours: Monday-Friday, 9 A.M.-6 P.M.; Saturday, 10 A.M.-5 P.M.
Admission free.

## BIOTECH BEGINNINGS: CUT-AND-PASTE GENES

In 1973, Dr. Herbert Boyer and Dr. Stanley Cohen conducted the first successful experiments in gene splicing, a facet of genetic engineering. These experiments eventually led to the multibillion-dollar biotechnology industry that began in the early 1980s.

The two California college professors and biochemists attended a U.S.-Japan joint conference on bacterial plasmids in Honolulu in November 1972. After listening to each other's presentations, Cohen, of Stanford University, and Boyer, of the University of California at San Francisco (UCSF), walked over to a local deli to discuss the possibility of a professional collaboration to further each other's research.

Boyer's paper on bacterial enzymes capable of cutting DNA at specific sites (restriction enzymes) intrigued Cohen. The Stanford University professor had already successfully extracted plasmids from cells and transplanted them into the cytoplasm of other cells. If, Cohen reasoned, he could incorporate Boyer's DNA-splicing technique into his own experiments, then perhaps he could transfer one organism's DNA into another to create a third organism.

By early 1973, the two scientists had begun a series of experiments they hoped would lead to a method of selecting and replicating specific foreign genes in bacteria. The technique, now known as gene splicing, resulted in the first predetermined recombinant DNA. (Recombinant DNA, according to *Webster's College Dictionary,* is "genetically engineered DNA prepared in vitro by cutting up DNA molecules and splicing together specific DNA fragments usually from more than one species of organism.") Three research papers published by Cohen, Boyer, and colleagues at Stanford and UCSF in 1973 and 1974 demonstrated the method's use in replicating the DNA of both lower and higher organisms. Cohen followed up with a 1975 *Scientific American* article explaining the gene-splicing technique, its scientific usefulness, and its commercial potential for producing hormones and other chemicals once made only by the human body.

Seven years later, in December 1980, the U.S. Patent and Trademark Office issued the first of three basic gene-splicing patents to Stanford and the University of California. It was the first significant patent issued in the new field of biotechnology. Meanwhile, Cohen continued his scientific research, eventually winning the Nobel Prize in 1986 for his work with Rita Levi-Montalcini in discovering cell growth factors.

While waiting for the patent to be approved, Boyer cofounded Genentech with venture capitalist Robert A. Swanson in April 1976. At the time, Boyer was a biochemistry and biophysics professor at UCSF as well as director of the graduate program in genetics.

In April 1996, Boyer and Cohen were awarded the $500,000 Lemelson-MIT Prize "for their inventions, entrepreneurship, and the spirit of team-work which allowed them their success."

## First Biotech Firm

In 1978, Genentech researchers synthesized human insulin using the technique pioneered by Cohen and Boyer. When the company went public in 1980, it raised $35 million with an initial public offering of $35 a share that zoomed up to $88 in less than half an hour, one of the largest stock run-ups ever. Not until 1982, however, did the insulin—the company's first recombinant DNA product—reach consumers. Genentech had licensed this first product of genetic engineering to Eli Lilly and Company.

In 1997, in recognition of Genentech's establishment of South San Francisco as the site of biotechnology's beginnings, the city renamed the

One year after forming Apple Computer, co-founder Steve Jobs posed with the Apple II in 1977. The Apple II is considered the first ready-made personal computer. *Courtesy of AP/Worldwide Photos*

portion of the street where the company was located from Point San Bruno Boulevard to DNA Way, giving Genentech the appropriate address of 1 DNA Way.

## READY-TO-USE PERSONAL COMPUTER: APPLE WITH A BYTE

In April 1977, two Silicon Valley–raised computer nerds named Steve revolutionized the computer industry with their Apple II personal computer. Introduced a year after the partners incorporated their fledgling company, Apple Computer, the Apple IIs were, according to Len Shustek of the Computer Museum, "the first machines that somebody could take home

## WHY THE NAME "APPLE"?

Some say Apple Computer is named after the Beatles' record company. Others say Steve Jobs named it after his favorite fruit. Still others say that Jobs chose the name after spending a summer picking apples in Oregon.

In the words of Steve Wozniak: "You didn't have to have a real specific reason for choosing a name when you were a tiny little company of two people; you choose any name you want."

and plug into the wall and get working without a degree in electrical engineering. . . . It was really a breakthrough machine."

Former Hewlett-Packard calculator designer Steve Wozniak based the Apple II on his Apple I, which he and Steve Jobs had designed in Jobs's bedroom and built the prototype for in his family's garage. While the 600 Apple I machines sold ended up in the hands of engineers and computer hobbyists, the Apple II found its way into the homes of "regular" people, offices of small businesses, and many schools.

The Apple II debuted at Jim Warren's 1977 West Coast Computer Faire (WCCF) in a prime location near the entrance, thanks to Steve Jobs's forethought and finagling. There was nothing else like it at the show. With its color display, slots for add-ons, expandable memory capability, easy-to-control keyboard, and BASIC stored in its ROM chip, the Apple machine was a hit. In fact, following the WCCF, people began showing up at the company's tiny Cupertino office to watch biweekly demonstrations of the Apple II.

Though the computer was a collaborative effort between the two Apple partners, electronics wizard Wozniak is credited as the sole designer of the Apple II's inner workings, while marketing master Jobs gave the computer its appealing "look." With the financial help of venture capitalist Arthur Rock, who had funded Intel, and supervision from a former Intel manager named Mike Markkula, Wozniak and Jobs were able to have 1,000 Apple IIs manufactured at a local factory.

In its first three years in the marketplace, the Apple II, which sold for about $1,300 retail, made $139 million for Apple Computer. When the company went public in 1980, its stock rose from an initial public offering of $22 to $29 the first day, bringing the market value of Apple to about $1.2 billion.

Most computer-industry analysts believe the main factors that contributed to the phenomenal success of the Apple II were: its open system that allowed for add-ons; its inexpensive, Wozniak-engineered disk drive; the availability of Apple-compatible software that allowed non-programmers to use a computer; its attractive, clean packaging; and the computer's simple name.

Before the Apple II, nobody owned a personal computer. Within five years of its debut, however, California's Silicon Valley had become the hotbed of a billion-dollar-plus computer industry jump-started by Apple Computer.

# "Fun Fun Fun"
## Sports and Recreation

### BEACH VOLLEYBALL: SERVES, SPIKES, AND SANDY TOES

Of all the beaches in all the towns in all the world, why did beach volleyball begin in Santa Monica? Well, perhaps three miles of gorgeous Pacific Ocean coastline and 300 days a year of sunshine have something to do with it. More likely, however, it was the fact that someone installed the world's first beach volleyball courts on Santa Monica sands in the early 1920s. These first gritty courts attracted families who participated in six-against-six games for pure recreational pleasure.

In 1930, a Santa Monica beach became the venue for the first two-man beach volleyball game, and soon after, Depression-era Southern Californians flocked to the beach to play volleyball. Though the sport languished during World War II, it experienced a resurgence in the postwar period. In 1947, player Bernie Holtzman organized the first official two-man beach volleyball tournament, held at California's State Beach. While the winning team got the glory, the players didn't get a prize. The following year, organizers of the State Beach tournament awarded a crate of Pepsi to the winning team.

Beach volleyball took on a new life in the 1950s as the first open tournaments were held on five California beaches: Santa Barbara, State, Corona del Mar, Laguna, and San Diego. At the same time, the sport became a form of entertainment, with beauty contests included as part of the program. In a 1957 event won by Bernie Holtzman and Gene Selznick, an actress named Greta Tyson was crowned "Queen of the Beach."

By the 1960s, beach volleyball had become inextricably linked to the "California lifestyle" of beaches, sun, and rock music. It also began attracting publicity. The decade's star players included Mike O'Hara, Mike Bright, Ron Von Hagen, and Selznick, and tournaments were held on eight California beaches, including Lake Tahoe.

In 1965, the California Beach Volleyball Association (CBVA) was founded to coordinate schedules and define the game's rules, and in the 1970s beach volleyball went professional. The amount of prize money and the number of spectators increased as the decade progressed. Two hundred fifty people watched the first sponsored tournament in 1974, which offered $1,500 and took place in San Diego. Dennis Hare and Fred Zuelich won first place. Two years later, at the Olympia Championship of Beach Volleyball at State Beach in Pacific Palisades, 30,000 spectators watched as the team of Jim Menges and Greg Lee took the top prize. Prize money then totaled $5,000. Pro tournaments in Santa Cruz, Lake Tahoe, and Los Angeles followed in 1977, and the following year the sport's first major sponsor, Jose Cuervo Tequila, came on board. The decade closed with the first "King of the Beach" tournament in Manhattan Beach, with $11,000 in prize money.

Professional beach volleyball really took flight during the 1980s, beginning with the first sponsored tournament tour in the United States. As the decade flew by, the number of tournaments increased dramatically as Miller Brewing and Bolle Sunglasses signed on as sponsors, the USA tour went national, the Association of Volleyball Players (AVP) was founded, and the first international beach volleyball exhibition was held in Rio de Janeiro.

The first international beach volleyball tournament sponsored by the Federation Internationale de Volleyball (FIVB) was held in 1987 at Ipanema Beach, with the U.S. team of Sinjin Smith and Randy Stoklos winning. For the next few years, United States teams (Karch Kiraly and Pat Powers, Smith and Stoklos) won the FIVB men's tournaments, including the first FIVB World Series with Smith and Stoklos as 1989–90 men's world champions. Since then, the Swiss-based FIVB has been largely responsible for the growth of beach volleyball as an international sport.

The United States dominated international beach volleyball competition in the early 1990s with both men's and women's teams earning world champion titles. Notable U.S. players of the 1990s include Kiraly, Kent Steffes, Karolyn Kirby, and Liz Masakayan. Beach volleyball made its Olympic debut at the 1996 Atlanta Games, and the American men's team of Kiraly and Steffes won the gold while Americans Mike Dodd and Mike Whitmarsh took the silver. Since then, Brazilian teams have dominated the sport.

Today, as throughout beach volleyball's history, the vast majority of professional U.S. players, both male and female, come from or reside in Southern California's beach communities. Thus, California, the birthplace of beach volleyball, remains the breeding ground for America's players.

### VOLLEYBALL IN THE SAND—A CELEBRITY DRAW

President John F. Kennedy attended the first official beach volleyball event at Sorrento Beach, California; Marilyn Monroe talked about the sport in an interview; and the Beatles played a "game" on the Sorrento Beach sand.

## THE YO-YO: A NEW SPIN ON AN ANCIENT TOY

The yo-yo as we know it today was first manufactured in the United States by Pedro Flores. The young Filipino introduced the first yo-yo to have its string looped around the axle instead of tied to it. Before Flores's innovative design, the earlier version, known as the *bandalore,* could move only up and down the string. Flores's design change made possible the performance of a multitude of tricks, many still done today.

Flores moved to the United States in 1915, attended San Francisco's High School of Commerce (1919–20), and studied at the University of California at Berkeley and Hastings College of Law in San Francisco. Moving to Santa Barbara, he worked odd jobs, became a bellboy, then decided he wanted to be his own boss. Remembering the yo-yo's popularity in his native country, Flores found himself bitten by the entrepreneurial bug. On June 9, 1928, Flores applied for and received a license for his Yo-Yo Manufacturing Company. Initially, he hand-carved a dozen yo-yos and sold them to neighborhood children. Within five months, his company had produced 2,000 of the hand-carved toys.

In 1928, two Los Angeles businessmen, James and Daniel Stone, invested in Flores's yo-yo venture. Four months later, the company had machine-manufactured 100,000 yo-yos. Within a year, Flores and the Stones were running three factories employing 600 workers: Flores and Stone (Los Angeles), Flores Yo-Yo Corporation (Hollywood), and Yo-Yo Manufacturing Company (Santa Barbara).

Flores hired Dorothy Carter as his chief yo-yo designer, and she created a variety of designs for the company. Depending on the design and decoration, Flores yo-yos sold for anywhere from 15 cents to $1.50 in 1929.

### THE NAME "YO-YO"

The American public was introduced to the term *yo-yo* in a 1916 article titled "Filipino Toys" in a supplement to *Scientific American. Yo-yo* means "come, come" or "come back" in Tagalog.

Promoting his yo-yo as "The Wonder Toy" and using the slogan "If it isn't a Flores, it isn't a yo-yo," Flores set off yo-yo mania beginning in late 1928. In less than two years, his production had increased to more than 300,000 yo-yos a day. Flores also originated yo-yo contests, the earliest consisting of yo-yo-spinning endurance matches. However, most people attribute the beginning of the yo-yo craze to businessman Donald F. Duncan Sr.

Duncan, who was already successful at marketing the Eskimo Pie, the parking meter, and the movie screen, saw a youngster playing with one of Flores's yo-yos and recognized the money-making potential of the toy. In partnership with newspaperman William Randolph Hearst, Duncan helped Flores market his yo-yos. He arranged a deal with Hearst for free

### *YO-YO TRIVIA*

★ While playing with a yo-yo during the proceedings of the House Subcommittee on Un-American Activities in 1968, Abbie Hoffman was cited for contempt of Congress.

★ Presidents John F. Kennedy and Lyndon B. Johnson publicly played with yo-yos while in office.

★ Richard Nixon played with a yo-yo onstage at the opening of the Grand Ole Opry in 1974.

★ On April 12, 1985, the yo-yo became the first toy taken into space when it traveled on the space shuttle *Discovery* to test the effects of microgravity.

★ The yo-yo returned to space on July 31, 1992, aboard *Atlantis* for use in an educational video.

★ Yo-yo manufacturer Tom Kuhn constructed a yo-yo that weighed 256 pounds and measured 50 inches in diameter.

and low-cost advertising space for Flores yo-yos in Hearst's Northern California newspapers. In exchange, participants in Flores's yo-yo contests were required to sell newspaper subscriptions to pay for their contest entry fees. Around 1930, Flores sold his company to Duncan, who, in 1932, acquired the Flores trademark and began selling both Flores and Duncan yo-yos.

Flores did not retire from the yo-yo world after selling to Duncan. In fact, during 1931 and 1932, Flores helped set up several Duncan yo-yo contests around the country. In the 1940s, Flores assisted Joe Radovan in establishing the latter's Chico Yo-Yo Company. In 1954, Flores started the Flores Corporation of America to produce yo-yos. Though Flores's new company was a short-lived venture, Pedro Flores will always be known as the man who introduced the yo-yo to America.

###  To Visit: National Yo-Yo Museum

The National Yo-Yo Museum, located in Chico, features exhibits of the evolution and marketing of the yo-yo. Covering 80 years of yo-yo history, the museum houses the D. F. Duncan Family collection of Duncan, Cherrio, Festival, Royal, and Flores yo-yos. Also featured is the Dr. Tom Kuhn Collection, including the world's largest yo-yo. Visitors to the museum can view nostalgic photos of yo-yo campaigns and contests as well as historic yo-yo contest awards, patches, ribbons, and trophies.

**National Yo-Yo Museum**
320 Broadway (located inside "Bird in Hand")
Chico, CA 95928
530-893-0545
Hours: Monday-Saturday, 10 A.M.-5:30 P.M.; Sunday, 11 A.M.-4 P.M.
Admission free.

*"Flat flip flies straight. Tilted flip curves. Play catch. Invent games."*

Pluto Platter instructions

The evolution of the world's first plastic flying disc to "Frisbee" took place in three stages. Two former World War II pilots invented the prototype disc—the "Flyin' Saucer"—in the basement of a San Luis Obispo home. Then one of the partners, unbeknownst to the other, developed his own version of the toy in Los Angeles and patented it as the "Pluto Platter." Finally, the WHAM-O company of San Gabriel bought the rights to the Pluto Platter, renamed it, and then trademarked it "Frisbee."

Warren Franscioni had served as a pilot with the Air Transport Service in India during World War II. Son of the mayor of Paso Robles, California, Franscioni decided to settle in nearby San Luis Obispo upon his return. There, in partnership with George Davis, he established a butane company.

In 1947, another World War II pilot named Walter Frederick "Fred" Morrison approached Franscioni and asked him for a job. Morrison had flown 58 missions over Italy until he was shot down and then held prisoner in the infamous Stalag 13. At the time Morrison contacted Franscioni, the company was in need of someone to install home heating equipment. So Franscioni hired fellow veteran Morrison.

The butane business in postwar San Luis Obispo was not exactly booming, so Franscioni and Morrison decided to start another business on the side to help support their families. Perhaps because Morrison grew up the son of an inventor (his father had invented the sealed-beam automobile headlight), the two decided to create a unique new product. The former POW recalled that as a child growing up in Utah, he would sail the lid of a paint can through the air for fun. This wasn't unusual. For decades, especially during the Great Depression, children had been throwing pie tins, paint can lids, cookie tin lids, and basically anything they could find that would fly. It was cheap fun.

Morrison and Franscioni decided to design a "flying disc." Their first design, made of metal, exhibited some problems. It was dangerous to passersby, noisy when it hit the ground, and harmful to the catcher. According to Franscioni, the partners mutually decided to make the toy out of plastic, the material *du jour*.

First they tried Tenite (then used in toothbrush handles and eyeglass frames), but it proved unable to withstand constant crashing into the ground. The two then found a more pliable plastic that wouldn't shatter upon impact and could be formed in an injection mold. At the time, UFOs and little green men had captured the imaginations of Americans. The partners took advantage of this new obsession, and they attempted to change the pie-tin shape of their toy "into what we believed would be the best configuration of an injection-molded Flyin' Saucer." In 1948 the San Luis Obispo *Telegram Tribune* reported:

> Hundreds of flying saucers are scheduled to invade San Luis Obispo in the near future. Two local men, pooling their resources after the words "flying saucers" shocked the world a year ago, have invented a new, patented plastic toy shaped like the originally reported saucer.

Forming a company named Partners in Plastic (Pipco), Franscioni and Morrison contracted with a Glendale firm, the Southern California Plastic Company, to produce the Flyin' Saucer. Franscioni paid for the initial mold, and the company paid 25 cents per unit. Pipco then sold the toy through Woolworth's and other outlets at a retail price of one dollar.

Because the Flyin' Saucer's appeal was in its movement, it was necessary to show the toy in action. Realizing this, the partners put on in-store demonstrations (in a protective cage), and Morrison and his wife took the toy to country fairs and wowed the crowds.

Fred MacMurray, the original Absent-Minded Professor, tosses a Frisbee right out of the photo.
*Courtesy of WHAM-O, Inc.*

About 1950, Franscioni and Morrison even managed to convince Al Capp of "Li'l Abner" fame to feature the Flyin' Saucer in one of his comic strips. This national exposure should have boosted the sales of the toy, except the Pipco boys made a costly marketing mistake. Soon after the strip appeared, they decided to package it with the toy. Angered by the unauthorized use of his artwork, Capp threatened to sue Pipco if the company didn't compensate him. He demanded $5,000, a substantial amount of money for the fledgling company. This event signaled the beginning of Pipco's demise and the partnership's dissolution.

Unfortunately for Franscioni and his family, the butane business went belly-up at about the same time. They were forced to sell the San Luis Obispo house where the Flyin' Saucer had had its beginnings. Franscioni found work as a truck driver and later reenlisted in the Air Force. In 1952, the family was sent to South Dakota.

Morrison moved to Los Angeles and became a carpenter and building inspector before starting his own toy company, American Trends. Intent on developing his own version of the plastic flying disc, Morrison came up with the "Pluto Platter." The new version looked a bit more like a flying saucer than the original Flyin' Saucer, with the outer third of the disc displaying a design feature later known as the Morrison Slope.

While demonstrating and hawking the Pluto Platter in downtown Los Angeles one day in late 1955, Morrison was approached by two recent University of Southern California graduates who had started their own toy company, WHAM-O. Recognizing the flying disc's potential, Richard "Rich" Knerr and Arthur "Spud" Melin brought Morrison into the company.

At the time, Franscioni did not know that Morrison had taken their toy, changed the name, and made a few design changes. So he was understandably baffled when, in 1956, he attempted to file for a patent on the Flyin' Saucer (referred to as the "aerial sounding toy" in his patent documents) but Morrison refused to sign the papers. The truth was that Morrison had applied for his own patent on the Pluto Platter (or "flying toy," according to his patent) and had withheld this information from his former partner.

WHAM-O's Pluto Platter went into production in San Gabriel on January 13, 1957, yet Morrison continued to collect sales commissions from the Southern California Plastic Company for the Flyin' Saucer. When the company president discovered what Morrison was doing, he cut all business ties with him and wrote a letter to Franscioni about his former partner's reprehensible activities. Though infuriated, Franscioni did not pursue a lawsuit. He was far from Los Angeles, attempting to reestablish his career, and the toy's potential earnings just didn't seem worth the time and trouble. (Southern California Plastic continued to manufacture the Flyin' Saucer, sell it at Disneyland and a few other outlets, and send Franscioni royalty checks until the mid-1960s.)

Meanwhile, Rich Knerr of WHAM-O had undertaken a Pluto Platter promotional tour of East Coast college campuses. While visiting Yale, he observed students tossing Frisbie Pie Company pie tins and cookie tin lids across long distances to each other as if they were Pluto Platters. Every time a student would toss a tin, he would yell, "Frisbie!" Knerr soon learned from the students that they were "Frisbie-ing." He liked the name so much, he returned to California and rechristened the Pluto Platter the "Frisbee." The Frisbie Pie Company closed down its operations in 1958, and on May 26, 1959, Frisbee became a registered trademark of WHAM-O. A world-wide craze that continues to this day had begun.

## THE ANT FARM: A LIVING TOY

Since its introduction about 45 years ago, the Ant Farm has become a staple of the American toy industry as well as a baby boomer icon. It seems natural that the idea for a toy involving ants would materialize during a picnic, and that's exactly what happened in 1956. Milton Levine was attending a Fourth of July backyard picnic at his sister's San Fernando Valley home when he noticed that "the kids were more interested in lying around and watching anthills than swimming in the pool." Soon the transplanted

"Uncle" Milton Levine poses with a Giant Ant Farm, one of several ant-related toys produced by his Westlake Village–based company. *Courtesy of Uncle Milton Industries, Inc.*

Pittsburgh resident found his own attention drifting to the ants, a sight that set off a rush of childhood memories for the 42-year-old: "It sort of woke me up to the fact that when I was a kid, I used to go to my uncle's farm in Pennsylvania and fool around with ants. We'd put 'em in a Mason jar with a little dirt and watch 'em cavort."

Levine, who already owned and operated a novelty toy mail-order business featuring spud guns, rubber shrunken heads, and miniature toy soldiers, thought: "Why not make an item that people could see through . . . one that was flatter, that people could see most of the tunnels . . . and make it reasonable?"

Levine placed a two-inch advertisement in the *Los Angeles Times* that beckoned would-be ant enthusiasts to "watch the ants dig tunnels and build bridges" in their own "Ant Farms." Soon after the ad appeared, orders for the $2.98 Ant Farm, the first "toy" of its kind, deluged Levine's already successful business. The backdrop of the original six-by-nine-inch plastic Ant Farm looked like a regular farm, complete with barn, farmhouse, windmill, and silo. "Uncle" Milton Levine, who has said that the farm idea came from a coloring book, credits the farm scene with the toy's early success.

Just as with the Original Ant Farm, today each Uncle Milton's Ant Farm comes with an "Ant Watchers' Manual" and a mail-in "stock certificate" to send to Uncle Milton Industries for vials of California red ants (*Pogonomyrmex californicus*). Because shipping queen ants is illegal, and male ants just mate and die, the company sends female harvester ants upon receipt of the certificate. Unable to reproduce, the colony usually lives only three or four months in the Ant Farm.

---

### WHY "UNCLE" MILTON?

"Everyone always said, 'You've got the ants, but where's the uncles?' So I became Uncle Milton."—Milton Levine

By the beginning of the 21st century, Uncle Milton Industries had sold 18 million Ant Farms and more than 500 million ants. The Ant Farm's popularity can be confirmed by the number of times it has been shown or mentioned in motion pictures (*Beetlejuice, Parenthood, When Harry Met Sally, UHF, Short Circuit*) and television shows (*You Bet Your Life, Roseanne, Alf, Pee-Wee's Playhouse, The Cosby Show, Punky Brewster, Dr. Who, The Wonder Years, The Munsters*).

Until 1992, all Ant Farms were assembled in shelter houses for the disabled, but since then the majority have been manufactured in China. Only the Giant Ant Farm and the Ant Farm Bonus Pack are manufactured in Los Angeles.

Today, Westlake Village–based Uncle Milton Industries has diversified its product line, though the Ant Farm in various forms is still a big seller. In addition to the Original Ant Farm (now available in four colors), Uncle Milton sells the Giant Ant Farm, the Mini Ant Farm, Antville, Ant Farm Village, and Ant Worlds.

## Where Do They Get All Those Ants?

Uncle Milton's ant catchers have found California's Mojave Desert fertile ground for harvesting *Pogonomyrmex californicus*. One of Uncle Milton's early ant catchers, Kenneth Gidney, began providing insect stock for Ant Farms in 1959. When he retired, the father of 10 passed on his trade to his daughter Robin Brenner.

There are various techniques for catching ants. Some ant catchers use straws to blow air at ants and then catch them as they flee. Brenner's technique was to use a car vacuum connected to a Tupperware container. While the company will not disclose how much it pays its few ant catchers, in 1990 Brenner was paid about $550 over a 10-hour period to gather 50,000 ants.

Once the insects are captured, workers fill small vials with 30 ants each before shipping them to Ant Farm owners. To prevent the tiny creatures from spending the weekend in a post office, ants are shipped on Mondays only.

California surfers, frustrated when the surf wasn't up, created the first "modern" skateboards and the sport of skateboarding in the 1950s as a way to pass the time and have fun while waiting for waves. Attaching the metal bases and wheels of roller skates to two-by-fours, Golden State wave riders transformed themselves into sidewalk surfers.

The first commercially manufactured skateboards, made by roller skate companies, appeared in 1959. Soon private California labels such as Makaha, Hobie, and Val Surf began producing boards.

When Los Angeles County lifeguard and surfer Larry Stevenson started promoting skateboarding through his *Surf Guide* magazine in the early 1960s, the sport increased in popularity. Stevenson's 1963 Makaha boards, the first professional skateboards, and his formation of the first professional skateboarding team further contributed to the sport's rapid growth.

The first skateboarding contest took place in 1963 in Hermosa at Pier Avenue Junior School and was followed two years later by the First International Championships. ABC's *Wide World of Sports* broadcast the event from Anaheim's La Palma Stadium, thus providing wide exposure and some measure of legitimacy.

Skateboarding's first wave crashed in the fall of 1965 due to inferior equipment, safety concerns, banning of the sport in several cities, and an overstock of inventory. Through it all, though, diehard skaters continued to skate and skateboard designers continued to innovate.

First, Larry Stevenson added a kicktail to his boards. Then, in 1970, Frank Nasworthy, from the San Diego area, introduced the Cadillac Urethane wheel and "single-handedly changed skateboarding forever," according to skater Eric "Arab" Groff in an article titled "Skateboard Heyday Was the 1970s." As Groff wrote: "This new product set the stage for skateboards to go above and beyond where they had been before with pool riding, downhill slalom, pipes, ramps, parks and sidewalks." In 1973, skateboard-specific trucks first appeared, and a couple of years later came precision bearings. The 1970s became skateboarding's second boom period.

In Southern California, specific areas became known as the territory of certain groups of skaters. While the Santa Monica–Venice area had the Z-boys of Dogtown, San Diego skaters were referred to as the Down Southers, and Upland/Claremont skaters became known as the Badland Boys.

Skateboarding moves of the 1960s imitated surfing maneuvers, but in the 1970s skaters created their own style, moves, and tricks. The most basic, the "Ollie"—invented by Alvin Ollie Gelfand—involves leaping into the air without the feet losing contact with the board.

After perfecting their moves in empty swimming pools and giant sewer pipes, freestyle skaters began skating and competing at specially built skateparks. Surfers World in Anaheim and Carlsbad Skatepark in Carlsbad were among the first such venues. Soon skateparks sprang up nationwide, but when liability-insurance costs became prohibitive, owners bulldozed about 80 percent of them. Though the sport went into hibernation again, committed skaters continued to skate on homemade backyard ramps as well as on streets and sidewalks.

In 1981, *Thrasher*, a gritty, hard-core skater magazine based in San Francisco, was launched to help diehard skaters stay connected to the skateboarding scene. A year later, Tony Hawk, perhaps the best vertical skater of all time, won his first contest at the Del Mar Skate Ranch. (Eighteen years later, Hawk made skateboarding history at ESPN's Fifth Summer X-Games in San Francisco when he successfully executed a "900," consisting of $2\frac{1}{2}$ rotations in the air above the halfpipe or vert ramp.)

With vertical skating on the wane in the 1990s, there was a resurgence in streetstyle, with skaters utilizing curbs, ledges, steps, handrails, and walls to test their skills. Some skateparks built in the last decade of the 20th century and at the beginning of the 21st incorporated street-like apparatuses to accommodate the new breed of skaters.

In addition, hundreds of skateboard manufacturers and allied companies have turned the sport into a $500 million business. And, true to skateboarding's California roots, out of the 340 manufacturers and distributors of skateboard decks, wheels, trucks, bearings, safety equipment, and shoes listed on the Skateboarding.com Web site, 225 of them are based in California.

Today, 1 in 10 U.S. teens owns a skateboard, there are more than 10 million skateboarders in the United States, and California boasts nearly 50 skateparks. In addition, skateboarding ranks as America's sixth-largest recreational sport and the third most popular among 6-to-18-year-olds. And to think it all started when the surfers couldn't get the Pacific Ocean to cooperate!

## THE HULA HOOP: FAD-O-RAMA

When the WHAM-O Manufacturing Company of San Gabriel introduced its Hula Hoop in 1958, the hoop had already undergone several incarnations over a period of 3,000 years. Ancient Egyptians and 14th-century English children had similar hoop toys, and 19th-century British sailors visiting the Hawaiian Islands noted similarities between the native hula dance and the movement hoopers made to keep a hoop spinning.

In 1957, the peak year of the baby boom, WHAM-O's Richard "Rich" Knerr and Arthur "Spud" Melin heard about a bamboo hoop Australian children used in gym class. The same year, an Australian manufacturer began producing and selling hoops made of wood. Knerr and Melin recognized the potential play and dollar value of the toy hoop. Reasoning that bamboo or wood would be impractical from both a production and a performance perspective, the WHAM-O founders looked for another material. They needed a lightweight and durable plastic. They discovered

### HOLD THAT HOOP!

In the late 1950s, Japanese officials banned use of the Hula Hoop in public because they feared that the mass gyration of hips could lead to impropriety.

Whether using a Hula Hoop in place of a jump rope or sending it spinning around the waist, suburban baby boomers turned the simple toy into a worldwide fad in the late 1950s. *Courtesy of the Security Pacific Collection/Los Angeles Public Library*

Phillips Petroleum, a chemical company that had developed polypropylene in 1951 and, a bit later, high-density polyethylene (HDPE), both types of Marlex plastic.

In 1958, Knerr and Melin traveled the Southern California playground circuit, demonstrating their "Hula Hoop" and giving away the toy. This marketing effort paid off, and children got hooked on the hoop. Not only did they swirl it around their waists, necks, arms, wrists, and ankles, but they also jumped through it and used it in place of a jump rope. It wasn't unusual to see someone twirling several hoops at one time on various parts of his or her body.

Promoted on *The Dinah Shore Chevy Show* and exposed nationally for the first time on *The Ed Sullivan Show* with Georgia Gibbs's rendition of "The Hula Hoop Song," the Hula Hoop grew from a Southern California phenomenon to an international craze. Within four months of introducing the Hula Hoop, WHAM-O had sold more than 25 million of them. Soon after, nearly 100 million overseas orders swamped the relatively small company. So great was the demand for the plastic toy that some crazed consumers hijacked delivery trucks full of hoops. As 1958 came to a close, the Hula Hoop had generated $45 million in profits. Not bad for a toy that sold for $1.98 retail.

By about 1960, the fad had died out, but WHAM-O, now with headquarters in San Francisco, continues to manufacture Hula Hoops in "three bright, swirly colors and three hoop sizes." The fad may have faded, but the toy lives on.

## AMERICA'S FIRST FASHION DOLL—BARBIE

Barbie, conceived and developed in Southern California, turned 40 years old in 1999. During her plastic lifetime, she has had 75 careers, has represented 45 nationalities, and has been marketed in more than 100 countries.

In pre-Barbie America, there were baby dolls, rag dolls, homemade dolls, and paper dolls. Only the paper ones represented adult figures with wardrobes approximating real apparel. Unfortunately, a child had to be dexterous enough with a pair of scissors to cut out the paper wardrobe, and the fragile outfits often tore.

Mattel's earliest Barbie dolls broke the mold in the doll world. Marketed by the Southern California toy company as the "Teen-Age Fashion Model" at the 1959 Toy Fair in New York City, Barbie was the first American fashion doll. *(BARBIE is a trademark owned by and used with the permission of Mattel, Inc.)* © *2000 Mattel, Inc. All Rights Reserved.*

In the late 1950s, Ruth Handler, co-owner of the Mattel toy company (then based in Hawthorne), entered the doll arena. A few years earlier, Handler had noticed that her daughter Barbara (nicknamed "Barbie") preferred paper dolls over baby dolls. They seemed to capture her imagination and help her create a fantasy world that included a closet full of the latest teen and adult fashions. Handler wondered if a three-dimensional "fashion doll" would appeal to young girls.

While on a trip to Switzerland, Handler discovered a leggy, buxom, 11-inch-tall doll named Lilli that was based on a character in a German comic strip. Though marketed in Europe as a "plaything" for adult men, Lilli became the inspiration for Mattel's Barbie doll (named after Handler's daughter). When the Handlers returned to the United States with a few Lilli dolls, the Mattel designers set to work to develop a prototype for America's first fashion doll, eventually generating a number of designs.

In 1959, Mattel introduced Barbie, the "Teen-Age Fashion Model," at the annual Toy Fair in New York City. Toy-industry buyers grossly underestimated the doll's sales potential. Thanks to television advertising, American girls *had* to have Barbie.

When the first Barbie hit retail stores in 1959, girls went wild for the $11^1/_2$-inch, ponytailed, adult-figured doll that sported a black-and-white-striped bathing suit, open-toed, high-heeled shoes, sunglasses, and gold-colored hoop earrings. The Barbie doll's red lipstick and nails and arched eyebrows accentuated her adult appearance. Mattel manufactured twice as many blonde Barbie dolls as brunette ones. In addition, the original Barbie had holes in her feet to allow her to be displayed in a two-pronged stand.

Since her introduction in 1959, Barbie has become a cultural classic:

★ Deemed a "symbol of the century," a Barbie doll was sealed in a time capsule in 1976 for the U.S. Bicentennial celebration.

★ Three years later, *Life* magazine featured Barbie in an article about 20 years of American fashion.

---

### BARBIE AS BABY BOOMER SYMBOL

During nationwide balloting in 1998, the American public selected Barbie as a subject suitable for a stamp saluting the 1960s. Among the other stamp subjects sharing the honors were: man walking on the moon, Woodstock, the integrated circuit, lasers, Dr. Martin Luther King Jr.'s "I Have a Dream" speech, the Vietnam War, the Beatles, the Peace Corps, *Star Trek,* Super Bowl I, the Green Bay Packers, Roger Maris, the peace symbol, and the Ford Mustang.

★ In 1986, Barbie made her float debut at the Macy's Thanksgiving Day Parade.

★ On September 17, 1999, the United States Postal Service issued the "Barbie Doll Stamp" as one of 15 stamps commemorating the 1960s.

★ Barbie played a supporting role in Disney/Pixar's *Toy Story 2*, released in theaters in November 1999.

★ As of the close of 1999, there were over 2,000 Internet sites featuring Barbie.

★ The list of Barbie licensees includes such products as girls' clothing and accessories, adult eyeglasses, cameras, Timex watches, the

The "Barbie Doll" stamp was one of 15 stamp subjects chosen by the U.S. public to commemorate the 1960s. *(BARBIE is a trademark owned by and used with the permission of Mattel, Inc.) ©2000 Mattel, Inc. All Rights Reserved.*

Barbie Rose by Jackson & Perkins, inflatable furniture, cake decorations and party supplies, and many more.

★ A mint-condition original Barbie will cost you approximately $5,000 (if you can find one). That's only about $4,997 more than the same doll would have cost you off the shelf in 1959.

Thanks to Ruth Handler's ingenuity and Mattel's marketing savvy, Barbie accounts for about $1.9 million in sales for the company each year.

## VIDEO ARCADE GAMES: BYE-BYE PINBALL

In a Sunnyvale watering hole named Andy Capp's Cavern, the video arcade–game revolution began with a volley of electronic Ping-Pong in November 1972.

One of Andy Capp's regulars noticed a strange machine with a television screen and a coin slot that November night. He inserted a quarter into the slot, a friend joined him, and soon they were playing PONG, which became the world's first commercially successful video arcade game. The machine's distinctive noises drew other patrons to it, and soon everybody wanted to play. Word spread overnight, and the following morning people were lined up at Andy Capp's to play the new and different game. About 10 P.M., the game suddenly stopped working when too many quarters caused the coin box to overflow and short-circuit the printed circuit board. It wasn't a flaw in the game that caused it to "die"; rather, it was its popularity. It was quickly repaired and put back into play.

Actually, PONG was not the first video game. Nolan Bushnell, considered the "father of the video arcade game," developed PONG along with engineer Alan Alcorn after Bushnell's first attempt at introducing a video game to the public proved unsuccessful. While a student at the University of Utah, Bushnell had enjoyed playing SpaceWar, developed by Steve Russell at MIT in the late 1950s. That game, created on a PDP-1 computer, used a cathode-ray-tube screen and an analog display. It was the first *computer* game; it was not a *video* game.

After graduating from college and not landing his dream job as a research engineer with the Walt Disney Company, Bushnell moved to Santa Clara County and became an engineer at the electronics firm of Nutting and Associates. In 1970, while at Nutting, Bushnell developed the world's first video game—Computer Space. It was a coin-operated, somewhat simplified video version of SpaceWar that used a mini-computer linked to a television monitor. The game made its public debut in 1971 but was too complicated for non-engineers to play. In addition to not understanding the instructions, people had trouble manipulating four different controls. Computer Space crashed in public.

Bushnell left his job at Nutting and Associates and, with $250 of his own money and $250 from his friend and partner Ted Dabney, he started his own business. At first he wanted to name it Syzygy (because he found the word in the dictionary and liked the fact that it had no vowels), but the name was already taken. Instead, Bushnell ended up calling the company Atari, from the Japanese strategy game "Go" in which a player says *"atari"* just before conquering his opponent (similar to

### A NEW CORPORATE CULTURE

Nolan Bushnell can be credited as the founder of a new type of corporate culture, especially in the engineering world of the early 1970s. He was not the typical corporate leader, and he did not hire corporate "types." Popular-culture writer Michael J. Weiss described the working atmosphere at Atari: "Engineers worked long hours, spurred on by piped-in rock. They held two- and three-day brainstorming sessions fueled by ample quantities of beer and pot. They gathered in 'think tanks,' the company's hot tubs. Many were, in Bushnell's words, 'interested in high technology for games rather than bombs.'"

"checkmate" in chess). The name was officially registered with the California secretary of state on June 27, 1972.

In May 1972, Bushnell had played a Ping-Pong-like game on an Odyssey TL200 computer at a Los Angeles Magnavox dealer. Ralph Baer, who calls himself the "father of home video games," had built what he referred to as his "Brown Box" (the first fully programmable, multiplayer video-game unit) in 1967 while working at a defense electronics company named Sanders Associates. Baer's video gaming system, which could be played on a home television set, was licensed to Magnavox in 1970. When Bushnell played the game in Los Angeles, it had just been introduced to the American market.

Admiring the simplicity of Baer's game and seeing its potential in the arcade market, Bushnell asked Atari engineer Alan Alcorn to design a Ping-Pong-like game in which an electronic "ball" could be bounced back and forth between two "paddles" that could be moved up and down. To motivate Alcorn, Bushnell made up a story that General Electric wanted the game. Thus, PONG, the first video arcade game, was created.

When Magnavox heard about PONG, about two weeks after its public debut at Andy Capp's, it demanded $700,000 for the rights to manufacture PONG coin-operated games. Bushnell's company responded by paying Magnavox a licensing fee under Baer's patents, and the game went on to

---

### ATARI EMPLOYEE NO. 40

Probably the most ingenious yet "different" Atari employee was the 40th one to be hired. He was a young, long-haired, hippie-like guy named Steven Jobs. With the help of his friend Steve Wozniak, Jobs developed the video game Breakout for Atari. Later, the two built their Apple I computer from parts left over from the Breakout project.

become a phenomenon. According to the Lemelson-MIT Program's Invention Dimension August 1998 "Inventor of the Week" article on Nolan Bushnell: "The games produced by Bushnell's company in the next few years . . . gave rise to not only the video arcade, but an entire industry that is still thriving today."

In 1998, sales of electronic games reached $5.5 billion. And it all began in a small Sunnyvale bar.

# "Eat It"
## Food and Drink

### THE NAVEL ORANGE: ITS RIVERSIDE ROOTS

The roots of the navel orange story stretch all the way to Bahia, Brazil, but credit for introducing the fruit to the North American public goes to an eccentric couple in the once-utopian colony of Riverside, California.

Luther Tibbets relocated from Washington, D.C., to Riverside in December 1870 and claimed squatter's rights. At the time, the town was a utopian community that had been founded by John W. North just a few months earlier. Argumentative and litigious, yet highly principled, Tibbets made few friends in Riverside. In fact, while embroiled in an argument over a grain crop, Tibbets's neighbor shot and severely injured him. When Tibbets erected a stockade with gunports from which to protect his corrals from thieves, the neighbors questioned his sanity.

While Tibbets finished setting up his homestead, his wife, Eliza, remained in Washington. Like her husband, Eliza had her eccentricities. She was obsessed with Queen Victoria and spent time trying to transform herself into the image of the queen. A Spiritualist, Eliza also participated in seances and various otherworldly activities.

When Eliza received word from her husband that John W. North was searching for the perfect fruit to grow in his new community, she contacted a Department of Agriculture horticulturist named William Saunders about any fruit trees he might have that could possibly flourish in Southern California. By coincidence,

Saunders had recently received a shipment of 12 exotic orange trees from a Presbyterian missionary in Bahia, Brazil. At the time Eliza contacted him, Saunders was seeking people to plant and cultivate the trees, which were known as navels because their seeds clustered at one end of the orange, thus giving it the appearance of the human belly button.

After Eliza moved west, Saunders sent her two of the Bahia navels. When she and her husband planted them sometime in 1873, nobody dreamed that these Brazilian oranges, later called Washington navels, Riverside navels, and ultimately just navel oranges, would start the California citrus industry in Riverside. But after about six or seven years of careful cultivation, the trees matured and yielded brightly colored, sweet-tasting, seedless oranges.

Once the Tibbetses' neighbors sampled the oranges at a housewarming party, everyone in the community wanted his or her own Bahia navel trees. To satisfy the demand and profit from their two trees, the Tibbetses sold the bud stock for up to $5 apiece. The trees became so valuable that Luther Tibbets erected a barbed-wire fence around them. News of the sweet, seedless, winter-ripening orange spread throughout California and the nation, and Riverside and surrounding communities became famous for their orange groves.

In 1903, the Tibbetses sold their Riverside property, and the new owner gave one of the famous trees to Frank A. Miller, who started the hotel that became the Mission Inn, and the other to the City of Riverside. Miller's tree, which Teddy Roosevelt helped plant while a guest at the hotel, died years later from overwatering. The city's tree, known as the Parent Washington Navel Orange Tree, is well tended in a small city park on the southwest corner of Magnolia and Arlington Avenues in Riverside. Designated California State Historical Landmark Number 20, the tree is the ancestor of most of California's millions of navel orange trees.

## ☀ *To Visit: California Citrus State Historic Park*

Located in the Arlington Heights area of Riverside, California Citrus State Historic Park preserves the cultural landscape of the state's citrus industry and relates the story of the industry's historical role in the development of California.

## California Citrus State Historic Park
9400 Dufferin Avenue
Riverside, CA 92516
909-780-6222
Hours: Call before visiting.
Admission free.
To schedule reservations for weddings, events, or meetings, call 909-352-4098 or 909-784-0456.
For more information, write to California Citrus State Historic Park, P.O. Box 21292, Riverside, CA 92516.

## CANNED TUNA: BEFORE CHARLIE AND THE MERMAID

If sardine schools off the coast of Southern California had not disappeared in the opening years of the 20th century, we may never have tasted tuna salad, tuna fish sandwiches, tuna casserole, or the infamous "tuna surprise." In fact, two beloved cultural icons—Charlie the Tuna and the Chicken of the Sea Mermaid—may never have surfaced.

In the late 19th century, a sardine cannery based in the San Francisco Bay area relocated to San Pedro and renamed itself the Southern California Fish Company. By 1903, for reasons unknown, local schools of sardines had disappeared, forcing company co-owner Alfred P. Halfhill to find another type of fish to can. After trying cod, halibut, and several other species and deeming them unsuitable for canning, Halfhill stumbled upon a tin of Italian "tunny." He hoped the "tunny," actually albacore (*Thunnus alalunga*), would save the company from financial ruin.

Unlike the sardine, albacore was abundant from Southern Baja California all the way up to the Canadian Charlotte Islands for about half the year. In addition, fishermen could catch albacore 20 to 100 miles offshore near the ocean's surface. Albacore was an abundant, relatively easy catch.

Halfhill immediately directed the cannery's foreman, Wilbur F. Wood, to find a way to prepare the albacore to make it look and taste palatable to the American public. Selecting only the best pieces of albacore, Wood began experimenting with precooking and steaming the fish. This process transformed the red fish meat into white meat that looked like chicken. Halfhill dubbed his new canned product "chicken of the sea" in part because of the albacore's appearance and texture and in part as a marketing tactic tying it to an already well loved food.

The Southern California Fish Company quickly processed and canned 700 cases of albacore and distributed them to grocery stores throughout the area. Unfortunately for the company, at first the public was reluctant to give the new and different product a chance. As a result, grocers shipped a large number of cans back to the cannery.

Knowing he had to come up with a marketing plan quickly, Halfhill decided to persuade grocers to give out free cans of albacore to any customer who bought coffee. The plan began to work, and Halfhill became convinced that someday his "chicken of the sea" would become a common food in the American pantry.

Several years passed. Then, during the World War I era, the companies that would eventually become Star-Kist and Chicken of the Sea established canneries in the San Pedro Bay area. In fact, in 1917 the Van Camp Seafood Company (now Chicken of the Sea International) became the first cannery to commercially pack yellowfin tuna. Thus, a mysterious act of nature and the prospect of looming financial disaster spurred one California businessman to save his company and inadvertently start a whole new industry.

## THE POPSICLE: MOTHER NATURE HELPS A YOUNG ENTREPRENEUR

One chilly night in 1905, 11-year-old San Francisco native Frank Epperson decided to fix himself a drink of flavored soda water. After stirring the soda powder and water with a wooden stick, young Epperson left the concoction, stick and all, on his front porch. As luck would have it, the temperature dipped below freezing that night, and the soda water froze around the stick. The following morning, the boy awoke to discover the frozen concoction and realized he had accidentally created a tasty treat. The enterprising young man began his entrepreneurial career by first sharing his frozen creation with his schoolmates and then selling it.

Less than a year after Epperson's serendipitous night of creation, the Great Earthquake of 1906 struck. While Mother Nature had lent a hand to young Frank Epperson one cold winter night, she now dealt a cruel blow to the residents of San Francisco. The quake and its aftermath of fires and floods destroyed almost the entire city and certainly sidetracked Epperson's entrepreneurial venture into the frozen-confectionery business.

In 1923, when Epperson was 29 years old, he applied for a patent for his frozen treat. The patent documents list the creation as "frozen ice on a stick." First naming the incredible edible the "Epsicle" (merging his surname and the word *icicle*), Epperson later changed the name to "Popsicle" because, according to newspaperman Al Sicherman, his own children called it "Pop's sicle."

At the time Epperson applied for his patent, he owned and operated a lemonade stand at an Alameda amusement park. Within five years, the lemonade salesman had sold more than 60 million Popsicles in seven assorted fruit flavors and had earned royalties for each Popsicle sold.

### POPSICLE STICKS

One of the benefits of eating a Popsicle is getting to the stick. Printed on it are riddles gathered and written annually by nearly 275 "riddle meisters." Popsicle sticks are great for crafts projects. And, according to Good Humor–Breyers, if you took the sticks from the more than 1.164 trillion Popsicle ice pops consumed in 1997 and laid them end to end, they would circle the earth three times.

In the 1930s, with the Great Depression eating into his profits, Epperson made the Popsicle more economical by creating the twin Popsicle. This "new and improved" version came with two sticks and enabled two children to share one Popsicle for a nickel. (Epperson also invented the Fudgsicle, the Creamsicle, and the Dreamsicle.)

Until the 1950s, Popsicles could be purchased only from the ice cream man. Then, as the baby boom progressed, grocery stores began selling them in multipacks. Today, Good Humor–Breyers owns the Popsicle line of products and offers more than two dozen Popsicle products in a variety of flavors, colors, and shapes.

## THE BOYSENBERRY: MR. BOYSEN'S HYBRID

When the City of Anaheim commissioned noted landscape architect Florence Yoch to design a 19-acre park in 1920, she recommended 25-year-old California horticulturist Rudolph "Rudy" Boysen to supervise the park's planting and maintenance. While Boysen was working at his Pearson Park duties, which ranged from raising all the flowers in a greenhouse to planting a cactus garden from specimens he'd gathered in the California desert, he was also developing a new strain of berry on the side. Within a few years, he had created a hybrid berry that would later bear his name.

Boysen had successfully crossed a red raspberry, a loganberry, and a blackberry to create a new purple-red berry that was shaped like a large raspberry but had a sweet-tart flavor. The plant grew like a trailing blackberry, but its drupelets (tiny, individual sections) were larger.

Boysen was unable to make the berry plants thrive on his farm, so he let them wither on the vine. Though he considered his experiment a partial failure, Boysen continued in the horticultural field, remaining with the Anaheim Parks Department for 38 years.

When Buena Park berry farmer Walter Knott heard the Anaheim park superintendent boast about the huge berry he had developed, he had to see

While Rudy Boysen created the berry that bears his name, it was Walter Knott who made the plants grow. Here Walter and Cordelia Knott stand in front of their Knott's Berry Farm boysenberry stand, where they sold the juicy berries for five cents a basket. *Courtesy of KNOTT'S BERRY FARM: ©2000 Knott's Berry Farm*

it. Upon visiting Boysen's abandoned fields, he took home six dying plants and, with the owner's permission and his own berry-growing expertise, nurtured them back to health. From these original boysenberry plants would grow America's first themed amusement park (see page 148).

## POTATO CHIPS IN A BAG: LAURA SCUDDER

*"My fellow Americans, I believe that the quality of life in America today is deteriorating because of the presence in our homes of canned potato chips. . . . When we were children, were potato chips packed in*

*an airtight can? No, potato chips were meant to be free—BORN FREE—bouncing around in a little bag."*

Mark Russell, political commentator and humorist, 1975

Laura Clough Scudder and her husband, Charles, began their potato chip business in the Los Angeles County community of Monterey Park in 1926. The Scudders, who constructed a brick chip "factory" next to their home, did not invent the potato chip. In fact, by the time the couple set up shop, about 25 other American companies were already involved in making the salty, crispy snack food. Laura Scudder did, however, revolutionize the chip biz by changing the way potato chips were packaged and sold to the public.

For nearly 75 years, potato chips were served mainly to diners in restaurants, or to picnickers by the local grocer, who scooped up chips stored in cracker barrels, glass jars and display cases, or metal boxes. Laura Scudder decided to sell her chips prepackaged in wax-paper bags ("flexible packaging," in packaging-industry lingo). Scudder's female employees would take home sheets of wax paper nightly. They would iron the sides, turning two sheets of paper into a single bag. The following day, the women would hand-pack Scudder's chips in the wax-paper bags and then seal the tops with a hot iron. This simple but unique new product—the potato chip bag—had a major impact on the chip industry.

In the 19th and early 20th centuries, food manufacturers delivered their goods to general stores or small shops in bulk. The consumer was left at the mercy of the shopkeeper as to his or her handling and measurement of the product. Scudder's prepackaging helped to protect consumers from unscrupulous shopkeepers, prevented the chips from spoiling, saved labor on the retail level, promoted safety and quality, and thus enhanced sales.

Scudder's Foods Company marketed "Mayflower" brand potato chips in Southern California and "Blue Bird" brand chips in Northern California. It also made and sold peanut butter. In 1957 Laura Scudder sold her business, but she continued to operate it until her death in 1959. The following year, the company moved to Santa Ana. Today, the Laura Scudder's brand is owned by the J. M. Smucker Company of jam and jelly fame, and flexible packaging is now a $17.5 billion industry.

## THE FORTUNE COOKIE: CHINATOWN'S AMERICAN ICON

The current incarnation of the basic fortune cookie—a baked confection of pastry flour (or cake flour), sugar, margarine (or oil), egg, and water folded around a small slip of paper with a printed prediction or aphorism—first appeared in San Francisco in the early 1900s. Then, in the 1930s, the cookie was "reinvented" as a gimmick to attract tourists to Chinatown.

After the Gold Rush, when the first Chinese residents settled the area, most non-Chinese San Franciscans and visitors considered Chinatown a ghetto. When the Great Earthquake of 1906 destroyed most of the city, however, wealthy San Franciscans rebuilt Chinatown, hoping to make it a tourist attraction. As Lan Cao and Himilee Novas state in *Everything You Need to Know About Asian-American History*, "Advertisements for Chinatown promised tourists an 'Oriental experience' in the Occident; a tour of Canton and the distant and magnificent land of Cathay." From the rubble of one of California's worst natural disasters rose a section of San Francisco resplendent in its eclectic mixture of Chinese and Edwardian architecture. Tourists began to view the area as a charming bit of the Orient in the midst of a bustling American city.

Local San Francisco legend has attributed the creation of the first fortune cookie to Makoto Hagiwara. Hagiwara, creator of the Japanese Garden in Golden Gate Park, is thought to have developed the cookie sometime between 1907 and 1914 as a tasty accompaniment to the tea served in his tea house. His "fortunes," however, were actually thank-you notes.

Meanwhile, Los Angeles baker David Jung, a Cantonese immigrant, claimed the cookie as his own creation when, in about 1910, he decided to place inspirational messages in cookies and hand them out to the homeless people around his shop. By the 1920s, Jung's Hong Kong Noodle Company was producing abut 3,000 cookies an hour.

According to journalist Michael J. Weiss, in 1983 the great fortune cookie case made it to the "Court of Historical Review," where a San Francisco judge ruled in a mock trial that the fortune cookie was a San Francisco invention. While Makoto Hagiwara's great-great-grandson believes his ancestor concocted the recipe for the cookie as we know it today, he also credits San Francisco's Chinese restaurant community for its part in building the cookie's popularity.

In 1935, when the Grayline tour bus company shuttled more than 10,000 tourists to and through Chinatown, the district's restaurant owners found themselves wanting for a dessert course for tourists who expected a sweet topper to their main meal. To accommodate this need, a Kay Heong Noodle Factory worker created the fortune cookie as we know it today. (Whether or not the baker followed Hagiwara's exact recipe is unknown.) The mystery remains as to how a cookie invented by a Japanese man ended up in Chinatown as a restaurant staple, but even Hagiwara's great-great-grandson agrees that Chinatown bakers, by devising a cost-effective way to bake the cookies as well as market them, ensured the fortune cookie's special place in North American culture.

Until the 1960s, when the first automated production of the cookie revolutionized the industry, the cookies were handmade. About a decade later, in San Francisco, Lotus Fortune Cookies' Edward Louie again improved on the cookie's production by inventing a machine that automatically inserted the paper fortune and then folded the cookie into its unique shape.

Recently, fortune cookies have been used as marketing, advertising, and public relations tools. No longer just an after-dinner delight, the simple fortune cookie has inspired customized and personalized versions, giant fortune cookies, fortune cookie bouquets, Scottish fortune cookies (baked with malt whisky, heather honey, and oatmeal) with slips of Scottish or Gaelic proverbs inside, one-pound gourmet fortune cookies, fortune cookies in several different flavors and colors, Jewish fortune cookies, fortune cookies containing New Testament Bible verses, and, believe it or not, fortune cookies for dogs.

## Ancient Beginnings

The fortune cookie most probably evolved from the centuries-old Chinese custom of celebrating festive occasions by exchanging Moon Cakes made from lotus nut paste. When China was occupied by the Mongols in the 13th and 14th centuries, the Chinese in Peking planned an uprising to rid their country of the ruling foreigners. To circulate information about the upcoming insurrection without having the Mongols discover their plan, the Chinese hid messages with the date of the revolt in the middle of their Moon Cakes (a delicacy distasteful to the Mongols). After a patriotic revolutionary disguised as a Taoist priest handed out the message-filled pastries to his people, the uprising ensued and proved successful. This hastened the beginning of the Ming Dynasty.

The tradition of giving message cakes gained popularity in China as a way of wishing good fortune to friends and loved ones on special occasions. Not until the mid-19th century, when Northern California's Chinese gold seekers and railroad workers celebrated the Moon Festival in their camps by exchanging biscuits with happy messages in them, did the

---

### VIRTUAL FORTUNE COOKIES

Cybersurfers can find some "virtual" fortune cookies on the World Wide Web. These two-dimensional treats, while impossible to eat, do have some advantages over "real" cookies: they are calorie-free; you have the option of clicking open a cookie until you find an acceptable fortune; and the variety of online fortune cookie sites covers the spectrum of philosophies and cultural trends.

precursor to today's fortune cookie appear in the Western world. When these former Forty-Niners and railroad builders settled in San Francisco's Chinatown, they brought the custom with them. Though it would be difficult, if not impossible, to authenticate, perhaps Makoto Hagiwara was familiar with this Chinese tradition.

### ☀ To Visit: San Francisco Fortune Cookie Factories/ Chinese Culture Center

San Francisco is home to: the Fortune Cookie Company of San Francisco, 728 Pacific Avenue; Lotus Fortune Cookies, 14 Otis Street; Chinatown's Mee Mee Bakery, 1328 Stockton Street; and Golden Gate Fortune Cookie Factory, 56 Ross Alley (between Jackson and Washington Streets). The Golden Gate factory encourages visitors to watch fortune cookie–making in action.

### Chinese Culinary Walk/Luncheon Tour—Chinese Culture Center

For an introductory experience to the food products and cuisine of China and Chinatown, including fortune cookie factories, consider taking this San Francisco Chinese Culture Center tour.

San Francisco's Chinese Culture Center
750 Kearny Street, 3rd Floor
San Francisco, CA 94108
415-986-1822
e-mail: info@c-c-c.org

## McDONALD'S: "SPEED, LOWER PRICES, AND VOLUME"

Brothers Richard and Maurice McDonald, better known as Dick and Mac, established the first McDonald's in San Bernardino in 1948. Although the brothers are rarely given the credit they deserve, marketing whiz Dick created the "Golden Arches" design and "Millions Served" signage, while operations specialist Mac (along with his brother) pioneered the concepts of preorder food preparation and kitchen as drill team/assembly line. In doing so, the McDonalds founded the world's fast-food industry.

In 1930, the young men moved from New Hampshire to California and first tried their luck in the fledgling motion picture industry, but instead found themselves pushing lights and scenery around Hollywood backlots. With the Great Depression just getting under way, the two opened a movie theater in Glendale. Unfortunately, they couldn't afford the rent. Closing up shop, they pondered their next move.

Looking for business opportunities, the brothers noted that Southern Californians were developing a dependence on their automobiles and that drive-in restaurants were beginning to dot the landscape to feed the mobile market. So Dick and Mac McDonald decided to open a drive-in restaurant. Though neither had any restaurant experience, they both believed the time was right for drive-in food service. The pace of life was speeding up, and a drive-in could provide food faster than a traditional sit-down restaurant could.

In 1937, Dick and Mac opened a drive-in hot dog stand just east of Pasadena. They prepared the food (hot dogs and milk shakes), waited on customers who sat on canopy-covered stools, and employed three carhops to wait on patrons in their cars. They did a modest business, but it was not good enough for them.

Three years later, the two brothers relocated to San Bernardino, a working-class boom town without a drive-in. Dick and Mac saw a market, and with a $5,000 loan from Bank of America, they built their first "real" McDonald's drive-in at Fourteenth and E Streets. From this 600-square-foot, octagonal-shaped building with a kitchen fully exposed to the public, Dick and Mac offered a 25-item menu featuring beef and pork sandwiches and barbecued ribs. By the mid-1940s, the brothers employed 20 carhops who served about 125 cars on weekend nights alone. The restaurant's annual sales amounted to more than $200,000. The brothers split the profits, which came to about $50,000 a year.

By this time, the McDonald's drive-in, like most drive-ins of that era, had become a teenage hangout. The carhops were slow and unreliable.

And to make matters worse, other drive-ins were opening in the area. Feeling the heat of competition and unhappy with their clientele and employees, Dick and Mac seriously considered closing McDonald's and opening a sit-down burger restaurant in suburbia. When the two pondered running a full-service restaurant, however, they realized it would be economically unfeasible.

The brothers began considering other options. First, they reviewed three years' worth of sales receipts and were shocked to discover that 80 percent of their business came from hamburger sales. They didn't need a 25-item menu with the time and expense it entailed. Believing they could make a lot more money through volume sales, Dick and Mac decided to take a huge gamble. They would close McDonald's temporarily and completely overhaul the business.

The first phase of the conversion process began in the fall of 1948. The brothers fired all the carhops and replaced their service windows with self-service, walk-up customer windows. Then they rearranged the kitchen and replaced the grill with two 6-foot-long grills to allow for optimum speed and for volume food production. Paper wrappers and cups took the place of flatware and china, making a dishwasher unnecessary. They reduced the size of their hamburgers from 8 per pound to 10 per pound. For speed's sake, they slashed their 25-item menu to 9 items. They also reduced their prices dramatically. Once 30 cents each, their burgers now sold for 15 cents. A slice of cheese could be added for 4 cents more.

When the restaurant reopened in December 1948, the menu consisted of hamburgers, cheeseburgers, three flavors of soft drinks in one size, milk, coffee, potato chips, and a slice of pie. All burgers came with ketchup, mustard, onions, and two pickles. The menu change allowed for streamlined production. According to Dick McDonald, "Our whole concept was based on speed, lower prices, and volume. . . . We were going after big, big volume by lowering prices and by having the customer serve himself." They installed an exterior sign displaying an animated, neon "Speedy" the chef and proclaiming: "McDonald's Famous Hamburgers. Buy 'Em By the Bag."

At first, the "new" McDonald's did not fare very well. Business was down, but six months into the postconversion period, after milk shakes and french fries were added to the menu, sales began to increase.

In keeping with the postwar baby boom, the McDonald's customer base shifted from teens to families with children, and Dick and Mac began targeting their advertising to the family market. The new McDonald's attracted adults by appealing to kids. Children were McDonald's boosters. They loved to watch their food being cooked in a big, shiny, stainless-steel kitchen. The brothers distributed promotional items to the kids, and they trained their countermen to be especially attentive to their youngest customers.

Yet the sales volume still didn't reach the level the brothers wanted. Undaunted, they launched phase two of their conversion: turning the restaurant into a well-honed assembly-line operation. They did for food preparation what Henry Ford had done for automaking. As John F. Love says in *McDonald's: Behind the Arches:* "The McDonald brothers had clearly developed a vastly different system, tailor-made for a postwar America that was faster-paced, more mobile, and more oriented to conveniences and instant gratification."

The brothers redesigned the kitchen to accommodate their new, "speedy" food-prep techniques. They also turned their crew into a drill team, each man a specialist. (Women did not work at the original McDonald's.) The new 12-man crew comprised three grill men, two shake men, two fry men, two dressers, and three countermen. Not having to hire short-order cooks saved on payroll.

To aid in quick, volume food preparation, Dick designed a special lazy Susan that held 24 buns. After the dressers added the condiments to the buns, they rolled the contraption on a portable platform to the grill men, who placed the burgers on the buns and then rolled the platform back to the dressers, who wrapped the finished product.

Dick wanted a machine that would produce hamburger patties of uniform size and shape, so he visited candy factories to see how their peppermint patty machines worked. At one factory, he found a machine that would produce the perfect patty with the push of a lever. When other custom-designed equipment was needed, Dick had local craftsman Ed Toman produce it. Among Toman's inventions were a hand-held pump that dispensed just the right amount of ketchup and mustard with one squeeze of the trigger and a very large, rigid spatula that the grill men could use to turn several burgers at once. Toman also modified the Multimixers used for milk shake preparation so shakes could be made in the cups in which they'd be served.

All the modifications finally resulted in the production speed and volume the brothers sought. By 1951, people would line up 20 deep in two lines during peak hours. That year, annual sales amounted to $277,000.

Now that the McDonald brothers had their production volume, they introduced another new concept to the food-service industry—preorder preparation. They would cook and wrap the hamburgers and fries before they were ordered as well as prepare and store up to 80 milk shakes in advance. This led to even faster service and a promise to fill orders in 30 seconds or less. It also resulted in strict health policies regarding when to discard food.

Meanwhile, Ray Kroc, owner of national marketing rights for Multimixer, wondered why a drive-in burger joint on the edge of the California desert had purchased 10 of his mixers. In 1954, desperately looking for a way to salvage his declining business, he decided to pay the brothers a visit and scope out the place. Kroc was amazed at the speed and efficiency of Dick and Mac's operation, as well as at the size of the crowd waiting in line to buy hamburgers. Kroc also noticed that every third order included a milk shake. (At around the time Kroc visited the San Bernardino McDonald's, it was serving about 150 customers at each lunch and dinner rush.)

Kroc saw tremendous potential for expansion of the McDonald's concept, but its owners did not care to exploit it. By that time, they had enough money to live well, and they didn't want the ulcers that can come with running a big business. Besides, both brothers were afraid to fly, and a McDonald's expansion would certainly have meant a lot of travel. They had sold a few franchises, mostly rent-a-name stores without any quality control or consistency. Kroc assured the brothers that he would do all of the traveling and assist with the running of the business. So, within a short time, Kroc became their franchising agent. On March 2, 1955, he formed McDonald's System Inc. (later renamed McDonald's Corporation), and about a month later Kroc opened his own McDonald's franchise in Des Plaines, Illinois. In 1961, Kroc bought out the McDonald brothers for $2.7 million cash, and he went on to become the innovator of a unique franchising system that took Dick and Mac McDonald's small restaurant and made it the largest food-service organization in the world.

Kroc, however, was not the one who came up with the 15-cent hamburger. He was not the one who invented the self-serve, walk-up concept. He was not the one who originated a fast-food preparation system that could serve the customer in half a minute. And he was not the one who created the "Golden Arches" and the "Millions Served" sign concepts. Those honors belong to the "real" founders of McDonald's.

## California's First Links in Restaurant Chains

*1919 to 1950*

- ★ **A&W Root Beer Restaurants** (founded 1919 by Roy Allen, Lodi)
- ★ **Bob's Big Boy** (founded 1936 by Bob Wian, Glendale; originally named Bob's Pantry)
- ★ **Carl's Jr.** (hot dog cart, operated from 1941 by Carl Karcher, South Central Los Angeles/Carl's Drive-In Barbecue, opened 1945, Anaheim/Carl's Jr., opened 1956, Anaheim and Brea)
- ★ **Hot Dog on a Stick** (founded 1946 by Dave Barham, Santa Monica)
- ★ **Baskin-Robbins** (founded 1948 by Burton "Butch" Baskin and Irvine Robbins, Glendale)

*1951 to 1958*

- ★ **Jack in the Box** (founded 1951 by Robert O. Peterson, San Diego)

The Cobb salad was created at Hollywood's famed Brown Derby. The eatery's whimsical architecture and its A-list patrons made the restaurant a landmark. *Courtesy of Teri Davis Greenberg*

★ **Denny's** (founded 1953 by Harold Butler, Lakewood)
★ **Shakey's Pizza** (founded 1954 by Sherwood "Shakey" Johnson and Ed Plummer)
★ **International House of Pancakes** (founded 1958 by Al Lapin Jr., Toluca Lake)
★ **Sizzler Steak House** (founded 1958 by Delmar "Del" Johnson and Helen G. Johnson, Culver City)

*1962 to 1985*

★ **Taco Bell** (founded 1962 by Glen Bell, Downey)
★ **Marie Callender's** (founded 1964 by Don Callender, Southern California)
★ **Coco's** (founded 1966 by John McIntosh, Orange County)
★ **Chuck E. Cheese's Pizza Time Theater** (founded 1977 by Nolan Bushnell, San Jose)
★ **Panda Express** (founded 1983 by Andrew Cherng, Glendale)
★ **California Pizza Kitchen** (founded 1985 by Rick Rosenfield and Larry Flax, Los Angeles)

### CORNUCOPIA OF FOOD FIRSTS

A number of culinary favorites were created or first served in the Golden State, including:

- ★ martini (1869, San Francisco or Martinez)

- ★ cioppino (1900, San Francisco)

- ★ chicken Tetrazzini (1908, San Francisco)

- ★ Crab Louis (1914, Solari's, San Francisco)

- ★ Green Goddess salad dressing (1915, Palace Hotel, San Francisco)

- ★ French dip sandwich (1918, Philippe's, Los Angeles)

- ★ Cobb salad (1937, Brown Derby, Hollywood)

- ★ double-deck hamburger (1937, Bob's Big Boy, Glendale)

- ★ mai tai (1944, Hinky Dink's, Emeryville)

- ★ Irish coffee (1952 or 1953, Buena Vista Café, San Francisco)

- ★ Rice-A-Roni (1958, San Francisco)

- ★ Ruby Seedless table grapes (1968, developed by Harold Olmo, University of California, Davis)

# "Up, Up and Away"
## Aviation and Aeronautics

## AMERICA'S FIRST INTERNATIONAL AIR MEET

After Reims, France, hosted the world's first aviation competition in 1909, American aviators Roy Knabenshue and Charles Willard considered the possibility of an international air meet held over American soil. Excited about the possibility, Knabenshue and Willard contacted fellow flier Glenn Curtiss to discuss the matter. Curtiss had been the lone American to participate in the Reims meet and had even won a prestigious trophy for reaching a flight speed of 46.5 miles per hour.

With winter putting a damper on East Coast and Midwest flying, the men believed that sunny Southern California would be the perfect location for the meet. Thus, Curtiss, Willard, and Knabenshue gathered in Los Angeles, where they met with Dick Ferris, a Knabenshue contact. Ferris, a businessman, civic booster, and aviation enthusiast, was to arrange financial backing for the venture.

Soon Ferris took charge of planning the event. Touting the benefits of the air meet for the Los Angeles area, he persuaded members of the Los Angeles Merchants and Manufacturers Association (LAMMA) to raise the necessary funds from community members.

After fund-raising, the first order of business was finding the perfect site for the event. So Curtiss, Willard, and the sponsors scouted the area and discovered a mesa on Dominguez Ranch, which was owned by Joseph and Edward Carson. The high bluff

By the end of the 1910 International Air Meet at Dominguez Hills, 11 airplanes, 3 dirigibles, and 7 hot-air balloons had competed. This photo captures some of the excitement of the event witnessed by a crowd that had probably never seen a plane in flight. *Courtesy of the Security Pacific Collection/Los Angeles Public Library*

would not only be good for the fliers but would also discourage nonpaying spectators by blocking their view.

LAMMA formed an aviation committee chaired by Ferris. The committee invited French aviator Louis Paulhan to participate in the air meet and enticed him to come by offering a guaranteed $50,000 if he competed. He accepted the offer.

Paulhan arrived in New York with two Blériot monoplanes, two Farman biplanes, his wife, their black poodle, and an entourage. Upon his arrival, he was slapped with a court injunction from the Wright brothers, who were claiming patent infringement for the Frenchman's use of lateral control wing design. Luckily for Paulhan and LAMMA (Paulhan was to be the meet's star attraction), the restraining order could not be enforced in California, and the Frenchman was able to participate in the meet.

By noon on opening day, January 10, 1910, about 20,000 spectators had arrived to see "aeroplanes" fly. Chances are that nobody watching had ever seen a plane in flight. Curtiss wowed the crowd when he took off in his yellow biplane, circled the course from about 50 feet in the air, and then landed in almost exactly the same spot from which he had taken flight. His maneuver signaled the start of America's first air meet. On the second day of the event, a growing crowd of spectators watched an amazing sight: in the air at the same time were one Farman biplane, two dirigibles, one Blériot monoplane, and one airborne balloon tethered to the ground.

As anticipated, the Frenchman upstaged the Americans. Paulhan set new records for altitude (4,164 feet) and endurance (1 hour, 49 minutes, 40

### *FIRSTS WITHIN A FIRST*

The 1910 Los Angeles air meet gave rise to several notable achievements:

★ Glenn Curtiss made the first successful airplane flight on the Pacific Coast when he traveled nearly a mile and was aloft about two minutes.

★ William Randolph Hearst took his first airplane ride, courtesy of Louis Paulhan, immediately became an aviation enthusiast, and later that year offered $50,000 to the first pilot to fly coast-to-coast within 30 days by October 10, 1911.

★ Lieutenant Paul Beck of the U.S. Army Signal Corps carried out the first bombing experiment from an airplane when, riding in a plane piloted by Paulhan, he attempted to hit a target with three 2-pound sandbags.

★ Mrs. Dick Ferris and Florence Stone became the first women on the West Coast to fly in a heavier-than-air machine when Paulhan took them on a flight above Dominguez Field.

seconds), for which he was awarded $14,000. Curtiss took home $6,500 for fastest speed with a passenger (55 miles per hour) and quickest start (covering 98 feet in $6^2/_5$ seconds). Charles Hamilton piloted hot-air balloons and dirigibles and performed spectacular airplane stunts to take home $3,500. Finally, Charles Willard's accurate takeoff and landing skills won him $250. By the end of the event, 11 "aeroplanes," 3 dirigibles, and 7 hot-air balloons had competed.

While the 1910 air meet proved profitable, it had more than a temporary monetary impact on the area. It started a long-lasting relationship between the aviation and aerospace industries and Southern California. Aviation and aerospace giants Douglas, Lockheed, Northrup, and Boeing have all established operations in the region.

In a somewhat prophetic closing-day speech delivered on January 21, chairman D. A. Hamburger of the Dominguez Hills Executive Committee stated:

> Certain it is that we have seen demonstrated before our very eyes that machines can fly. It only awaits the ingenuity and fertility of man's inventive and practical genius to make this mode of transportation a mercantile fact. The people of Los Angeles should feel proud that it was, and is, the only place in this broad land of ours where in the month of January the atmosphere is balmy, light, and warm enough to permit such a successful meet.

## LINDBERGH'S *SPIRIT OF ST. LOUIS*: SAN DIEGO–DESIGNED AND BUILT

Ryan Air Lines of San Diego constructed *The Spirit of St. Louis*, the first airplane to successfully fly across the Atlantic piloted by one man. The story of what is probably one of history's most famous airplanes began in 1919, when Raymond B. Orteig, hotelier and aviation enthusiast, offered a $25,000 prize for the first nonstop flight between New York City and Paris. News of a famous French aviator's unsuccessful attempt at winning the

Charles Lindbergh posed in San Diego with the Ryan Air Lines staff involved in building the *Spirit of St. Louis* shortly before the airmail pilot soared into the history books as the first man to fly solo across the Atlantic. *Courtesy of the San Diego Aerospace Museum*

Orteig prize in a Sikorsky trimotor with a three-man crew in 1926 spurred Charles Lindbergh, a skilled airmail pilot from St. Louis, to dream of taking the prize himself. Soon his dream turned into an obsession.

After hearing about a Wright Bellanca (a light, single-engine plane with an air-cooled American motor, designed for long-distance flight) at Columbia Aircraft in New York City, Lindbergh tried to buy it with $15,000 given to him by a group of wealthy St. Louis businessmen. The backers, who included the president of the chamber of commerce and the publisher of the leading St. Louis newspaper, trusted in Lindbergh's ability. Some of them had taken flying lessons from him. Plus, winning the coveted Orteig prize would be a public relations coup for St. Louis.

When Columbia Aircraft's chairman refused to sell the plane to the unknown airmail pilot because he wanted an aviator with a "name" to buy it, a disappointed Lindbergh returned to St. Louis. There he was hit with the news that more pilots had entered the competition. Still, his financial backers stood by their man. They had, in fact, gotten wind of an airplane manufacturer in San Diego—Ryan Air Lines—that would build a plane to Lindbergh's specifications. Upon hearing this, Lindbergh immediately boarded a train to California to meet with T. Claude Ryan, his partner, B. F. Mahoney, and their chief engineer, Donald A. Hall.

The first wholly Ryan-manufactured airplane was the M-1 (named in honor of Mahoney). The plane was produced for airmail contractors in response to the U.S. Post Office Department's dissatisfaction with its aging fleet of De Havilland DH-4s. Soon the company was rolling out M-1s and B-1 Broughams in substantial numbers.

T. Claude Ryan, who had learned to fly at the American School of Aviation in Venice, California, in 1917, was accepted into the U.S. Army Air Service cadet class of 1919 at March Field in Riverside. He flew forest patrol in the West until his enlistment ended in 1922, and then he moved to San Diego. He met B. F. Mahoney there and taught him to fly.

Ryan's first business venture—Ryan Flying Company—was followed by Ryan Air Lines, with Mahoney as partner. By the time Lindbergh appeared on the scene, Ryan had sold his manufacturing interests in the company to Mahoney but had agreed to stay on temporarily as company manager.

In February 1927, Lindbergh met with engineer Donald Hall, and the two immediately went to work designing the airplane that would turn a Midwestern airmail pilot into a world-famous hero. Sitting at drafting tables facing each other, the engineer and the pilot worked in sync. Lindbergh knew exactly what he wanted and needed, and Hall understood his vision. According to aviation writer Jon Guttman, "Lindbergh wanted three things to be observed in this order: efficiency, safety, and then, and only then, comfort." To this end, Hall and Lindbergh started with a standard Ryan M-2 (a strut-braced, single-engine monoplane) and transformed it into what was basically a flying gas tank.

Lindbergh feared losing his way and running out of gas, so he and Hall did everything they could to design the most fuel-efficient flying machine possible. The engine (a 223-horsepower, nine-cylinder, air-cooled Wright Whirlwind J-5C) was moved forward, the cockpit was moved back, and

Notice anything odd about the *Spirit of St. Louis*? The plane didn't have a front window! Charles Lindbergh had to use a periscope to look out the side window in order to see where he was going.
*Courtesy of the San Diego Aerospace Museum*

the fuel tank was placed at the center of gravity. In addition, the front windshield was eliminated. To see where he was going, Lindbergh had to either use a periscope or turn the airplane to look out the side windows.

In addition to his intense concentration on the plane's structural design, the pilot took extreme measures to lighten the interior load. Unlike his fellow competitors, he would fly solo. This would save about 50 gallons of fuel. He also eliminated fuel gauges, took the exact amount of drinking water he'd need, installed a lightweight wicker chair as a pilot's seat, trimmed the margins off his maps, and did not bring a parachute.

Amazingly, Hall, Lindbergh, and the Ryan crew completed the design and construction of the plane in just six weeks, and in late April 1927, they rolled out *The Spirit of St. Louis*. In exchange for their financial backing, the St. Louis group had taken the initiative of naming the plane. Also known as the Ryan NYP (for "New York to Paris"), the unique airplane displayed the San Diego company's name in black lettering.

Before heading to New York and ultimately to Paris and into the history books, Lindbergh executed several test flights at Dutch Flats in San

Diego. Then, on May 10, he took off for the East Coast. On the way, he stopped in St. Louis to thank his supporters. By the time he arrived in New York on May 12, Lindbergh had set a new record of 21 hours, 40 minutes for transcontinental flight. This was the first "first" for the Ryan plane.

When he landed on Long Island, Lindbergh was greeted with great skepticism by the press. Seeing the small, odd-looking plane with its wicker pilot's seat left many reporters questioning the man's sanity. Few believed he could survive the transatlantic flight, let alone complete it.

On the morning of May 20, 1927, Lindbergh took off from Roosevelt Field, barely clearing the ground and nearby telephone wires. Then, 33 hours, 30 minutes, and 29 seconds later, to almost everyone's astonishment, the American flier landed on the other side of the Atlantic. More than 150,000 people gathered at Paris's Le Bourget Field to witness history in the making. Not only had Lindbergh won the Orteig prize, but he had also become the first man to fly solo across the Atlantic. With this incredible feat, the San Diego–built Ryan NYP entered the annals of aviation firsts.

## AVIATION FIRSTS: REACHING FOR THE SKY

Golden State aviation firsts date from shortly after the Civil War and will no doubt continue throughout and beyond the 21st century. California's aviators, airlines, airplane manufacturers, test facilities, and abundance of talented and skilled engineers have all played a starring role in the history of aviation.

### 19th Century

*1869*

★ **Flight of a lighter-than-air vehicle in the Western Hemisphere**—On July 2, 1869, more than 30 years before the Wright brothers flew at Kitty Hawk, Frederick Marriott's *Avitor Hermes, Jr.* flew over South San

Francisco's Shellmound Park racetrack. The *Avitor*, which San Franciscan Marriott called an "aeroplane," was actually a 37-foot-long, cigar-shaped, dirigible-like craft with wings, a rudder, and a miniature steam engine. Aviation pioneer Stanley Hiller considers the *Avitor* "the first real airplane to fly. It had modern controls of pitch and yaw and tilt."

## 1883

★ **Successful glider flight**—After observing and studying seagulls soaring above Southern California's waters, John J. Montgomery became one of 19th-century America's foremost boosters of glider flight. Montgomery's 1883 flight in his *Gull Glider* near San Diego is recognized as the world's first successful glider flight.

## Early 20th Century

## 1904

★ **Successful controlled rigid-dirigible flight in America**—On July 29, 1904, Thomas Scott Baldwin piloted the 54-foot-long *California Arrow* over San Francisco Bay and back. The rigid dirigible's silk-covered framework carried Baldwin, who operated a 10-horsepower, 60-pound engine geared to a reversible propeller mounted at the front.

## 1911

★ **Shipboard landing and takeoff**—In January 1911, Eugene B. Ely flew his Curtiss biplane from Selfridge Field in San Francisco to San Francisco Bay, landing aboard the cruiser USS *Pennsylvania*. An hour later, Ely took off from the ship and landed on shore. Ely's landing on and takeoff from a naval vessel signaled the beginning of naval aviation and foreshadowed the modern aircraft carrier.

★ **Water takeoff and landing**—Piloting his Hydro, aviator Glenn Curtiss made history on January 25, 1911, when he took off from, and landed the plane on, the waters off North Island, Coronado, near San Diego.

- ★ **Naval aviator**—Lieutenant T. G. Ellyson became the first U.S. naval aviator upon piloting a Curtiss Pusher at San Diego on January 28, 1911, three days after Glenn Curtiss's successful water takeoff and landing.
- ★ **World's first airmail flight**—Former race car driver Fred Wiseman of Santa Rosa built an aircraft he referred to as "a kite with a motor in it" in 1910. About a year later, his February 17, 1911, flight made history as the first airmail flight in the world, according to the National Air and Space Museum of the Smithsonian Institution. During the flight, Wiseman flew about 12 miles from Petaluma carrying groceries, newspapers, and mail for delivery in Santa Rosa.

## 1913

- ★ **Woman to parachute from an airplane**—On June 21, 1913, over Griffith Field in Los Angeles, 18-year-old Georgia "Tiny" Broadwick became the first woman to parachute from an airplane when she jumped from Glenn Martin's plane as a publicity stunt cooked up by Martin.
- ★ **Inside loop**—Daredevil pilot Lincoln Beachey successfully executed an inside loop maneuver in a custom-built Curtiss craft over Coronado in November 1913. Beachey was also the first pilot to fly upside down.

## 1918

- ★ **Chinese American female aviator**—Bay Area pilot Anna Low was the first Chinese American female aviator.

## 1920

- ★ **Pilot issued reckless-flying ticket**—After demonstrating "reckless aerial driving" over Los Angeles on April 27, 1920, pilot Ormer Locklear was issued a citation and fined $25.

## 1923

★ **In-flight, plane-to-plane refueling**—Captain L. H. Smith and Lieutenant T. J. P. Richter took part in the first in-flight, plane-to-plane refueling above San Diego's Rockwell Field in June 1923.

## 1924

★ **Around-the-world airplane flight**—In a Santa Monica hangar, Donald Douglas constructed four Douglas DT-2s, two of which were successfully flown nearly 30,000 miles, leaving from Seattle and returning there in 175 days between April 4, 1924, and September 28, 1924.

## 1928

★ **All-passenger airline**—Harris "Pop" Hanshue, head of airmail carrier Western Air Express, used $180,000 from the Guggenheim Fund for the Promotion of Aeronautics to start a "Model Airway" specifically for flying passengers. Using 12-passenger Fokker F-10 trimotors featuring a mahogany-finished interior, a lavatory, stewards who served meals from a Los Angeles restaurant, and other amenities, his all-passenger service between Los Angeles and San Francisco, lasting 2 hours and 50 minutes, became the prototype for subsequent passenger airline service. Ironically, Hanshue was prone to air sickness and preferred not to fly.

## 1935–36

★ **Transpacific passenger flight and scheduled airline**—Pan American Airways' Martin M-130 *China Clipper* was the first plane to complete a commercial double crossing of the Pacific; it did so between November 22 and December 6, 1935. Only 12 passengers and 5 crew members made the historic flight aboard the large aircraft, which comprised a flight deck, one forward and two rear passenger compartments (each with eight seats or six sleeping berths), and a 12-passenger lounge. Nearly a year later (October 21, 1936), Pan American inaugurated regular transpacific passenger service, with the five-day flight originating in the San Francisco Bay area and making stops in Honolulu, on Midway and Wake Islands, and in Guam before reaching Manila (60 hours of actual flying time).

## World War II, Postwar Years, and Beyond

*1942*

★ **America's first jet aircraft**—Muroc Army Air Field in the Mojave Desert, renamed Edwards Air Force Base in 1950, has been a center of aeronautical testing and record-setting since Bell Aircraft's chief test pilot, Robert M. Stanley, and Colonel Laurence C. Craigie flew the XP-59A *Airacomet* there on October 1 and 2, 1942, respectively. The jet, built for testing purposes, is considered the ancestor of all American jet aircraft.

*1947*

★ **Helicopter airmail service**—Using a Sikorsky S-51, Los Angeles Airways began delivery of mail via helicopter on October 1, 1947, making it the first helicopter airmail carrier.

★ **America's first aircraft to break the sound barrier**—On October 14, 1947, Muroc Army Air Field once again became the site of an aviation milestone when Captain Charles "Chuck" Yeager (USAF), piloting the rocket-powered Bell X-1, exceeded Mach 1.06, or 700 miles per hour, at 42,000 feet—faster than the speed of sound. The plane, originally designated the Bell XS-1 and designed for a ground takeoff, was air-launched instead due to safety concerns. Yeager named the plane *Glamorous Glennis* after his wife.

★ **World's largest aircraft to actually fly**—Howard Hughes's HK-1 *Hercules*, better known as the Spruce Goose, boasts a 320-foot

Captain Chuck Yeager became the first man to fly faster than the speed of sound, a remarkable feat he accomplished in the Bell X-1 at Muroc Army Air Field (later renamed Edwards Air Force Base). Yeager named the jet *Glamorous Glennis* for his wife. *Courtesy of the National Archives, Still Pictures Branch*

wingspan, 17-foot-tall propellers, a payload capacity of 130,000 pounds (or 750 troops), and the option to be converted into a 350-bed hospital. On November 3, 1947, Hughes flew the eight-engine, plywood-and-birch aircraft over the waters off Long Beach, covering a distance of about a mile and reaching a height of 85 feet. After proving to his critics that the plane could fly, Hughes retired the wooden giant.

### 1953

★ **Airplane to exceed twice the speed of sound**—Douglas Aircraft Company of El Segundo developed the D-558 series of aircraft for the U.S. Navy to use in testing transonic and supersonic flight. With pilot A. Scott Crossfield at the controls on November 20, 1953, the D-558-2 *Skyrocket* reached 1,328 miles per hour over Edwards Air Force Base. This first plane to exceed Mach 2 was air-launched.

The metal shortage of World War II led the government to seek other materials, such as wood, to utilize in airplane construction. This was one of the reasons Howard Hughes began constructing his huge plywood-and-birch "Spruce Goose" (which didn't have any spruce in it). Unfortunately, Hughes finished building the plane after the war ended. *Courtesy of the National Archives, Still Pictures Branch*

*1954*

★ **U.S. jet fighter to reach Mach 2**—Manufactured by Lockheed Aircraft Corporation of Burbank, the F-104 *Starfighter*—known as "the missile with a man in it"—flew at twice the speed of sound on February 7, 1954.

*1959*

★ **Winged aircraft to achieve Mach 4, 5, and 6 and to operate at altitudes over 100,000 feet**—North American Aviation of Los Angeles construct-ed the rocket-powered X-15, the first winged aircraft to attain hypersonic velocities and operate at altitudes well above 100,000 feet. In 1959, during its initial test flights, the research aircraft bridged the gap between atmospheric manned flight and space flight.

*1986*

★ **Around-the-world, nonstop, non-refueled flight**—Taking off from Edwards Air Force Base on December 14, 1986, in *Voyager* and landing back there on December 23, pilots Jeana Yeager and Dick Rutan flew 24,987 miles in 216 hours, 3 minutes, and 44 seconds without stopping or refueling. The aircraft was designed by Elbert L. "Burt" Rutan, a native Californian who received his degree in aeronautical engineering from California Polytechnic University. *Voyager,* built and flight-tested over a five-year period, set a distance record for nonstop, global flight almost double the previous record set in 1962 and signaled the birth of a new generation of aircraft.

## VALLEY GIRLS IN SPACE: SALLY RIDE AND KATHRYN SULLIVAN

The first American woman in space and the world's first woman to walk in space have at least two things in common. Both were born in 1951, and both grew up in Southern California's San Fernando Valley. Even more coincidental, in 1984 they ended up on the space shuttle *Challenger* together.

Sally K. Ride, born in Encino, demonstrated intelligence and athletic ability at an early age. She was ranked 18th nationally on the U.S. junior tennis circuit, and after graduating from the prestigious Westlake School, she attended Swarthmore College before transferring to Stanford University. As an undergraduate, Ride majored in physics and English literature, receiving bachelor's degrees in both subjects in 1973. Continuing her graduate education at Stanford, she earned her master's degree in astrophysics in 1975 and her doctorate, also in astrophysics, three years later.

While working on her Ph.D., Ride read in the Stanford University newspaper that NASA was seeking candidates for its astronaut training

In June 1983, astronaut Sally Ride became the first American woman in space. She served as a mission specialist on the space shuttle *Challenger*. *Courtesy of the National Archives, Still Pictures Branch*

program. Until this time, NASA's astronaut recruitment efforts had focused on military test pilots. Now that the space administration was working with private industry, however, it had opened its candidate pool to scientists and technicians. Out of the original group of 8,000 applicants, NASA selected 208 finalists. After conducting intense physical and psychological testing and in-depth interviewing, NASA chose 35 individuals (6 of them women) for the program. Ride and Kathryn D. Sullivan were among them.

After joining NASA in 1978, Ride underwent a year of mission specialist training that included parachute jumping, water survival, flight training, radio communications, navigation, and adaptation to gravitational pull and weightlessness. Then NASA assigned her to the support crew for the second and third space shuttle missions, made her a mission control capsule communicatory (CAPCOM), and selected her as one of the designers of the remote arm for deploying and retrieving satellites.

In March 1982, NASA called up Ride for her first space shuttle mission. It was aboard the *Challenger,* in June 1983, that Ride became the first American woman in space. Twenty years earlier, female Soviet cosmonaut Valentina Tereshkova had won her place in the history books as the first woman in space. Then, less than a year before Ride's first *Challenger* mission, another Soviet woman—Svetlana Savitskaya—became the second woman in space.

On June 18, 1983, at 7:33 A.M. EDT, the *Challenger* blasted off from the Kennedy Space Center while hundreds of thousands watched. For mission STS-7, the shuttle's seventh mission, the *Challenger* carried a crew of five, and Ride was one of three mission specialists. During the six-day mission, Ride tested the remote robot arm that deployed and retrieved two satellites, assisted other crew members during take-off, ascent, and landing, and acted as flight engineer.

Ride's second mission also took place aboard the *Challenger.* The shuttle took off from the Kennedy Space Center on October 5, 1984, at 7:03 A.M. EDT. The crew of the 13th shuttle mission included Commander Robert L. Crippen, pilot Jon A. McBride, three mission specialists—Kathryn Sullivan, Ride, and David C. Leestma—and two payload specialists— Marc Garneau and Paul D. Scully-Power. The eight-day mission of STS-41G is remembered for two historic firsts: it was the first space flight to include two women, and Sullivan became the first woman to walk in space when she and mission specialist Leestma conducted a successful $3\frac{1}{2}$-hour extravehicular activity (EVA) to test the feasibility of the in-space refueling of satellites.

Sullivan grew up in the west San Fernando Valley community of Woodland Hills, graduated from Taft High School there in 1969, and earned a bachelor of science degree in earth sciences from the University of California, Santa Cruz, in 1973. She went on to receive her doctorate in geology from Dalhousie University in Nova Scotia, Canada, in 1978.

Sullivan, like Ride, officially became an astronaut in August 1979. In addition to her first assignment on *Challenger* mission STS-41G, Sullivan

Kathryn Sullivan and Sally Ride, both raised in the San Fernando Valley, ended up together aboard *Challenger* in October 1984. On this, the 13th shuttle mission, Sullivan became the first woman to walk in space. The shuttle flight also marked the first time in history that two women served on the same mission. *Courtesy of NASA*

served aboard the space shuttle *Discovery* on mission STS-31 in 1990 and on mission STS-45, the first Spacelab mission dedicated to NASA's "Mission to Planet Earth" program, in 1992.

Thus, two "valley girls," who grew up a few miles apart, went on to earn a place in history for their out-of-this-world firsts.

## OUT-OF-THIS-WORLD FIRSTS

Due to its climate, its wealth of engineering expertise, and the Jet Propulsion Laboratory in Pasadena, California has been involved in the development, manufacture, and operation of several spacecraft, from unmanned satellites to the space shuttle. Here are some of the state's "Space Age" firsts:

### 1958

★ **Successful U.S. satellite**—NASA launched *Explorer I* on January 31, 1958, in reaction to the Soviets' successful *Sputnik* satellite. The Jet Propulsion Laboratory in Pasadena operated the *Explorer I* satellite mission that provided evidence that intense bands of radiation surround Earth. This marked the first major scientific discovery to result from the space race.

## 1962

★ **American spacecraft to orbit the earth**—Los Angeles area–based McDonnell Aircraft Corporation designed and built for NASA the *Friendship 7* Mercury spacecraft in which John H. Glenn Jr. circled the earth three times during a 4-hour-and-55-minute flight. *Friendship 7* was the first American spacecraft to orbit the earth.

## 1969

★ **Manned lunar landing mission**—July 16 to July 24, 1969, marked a major milestone in space exploration when the *Apollo 11* command module *Columbia* landed on the moon, delivered the lunar module *Eagle* to its surface, and made possible Neil Armstrong's historic first steps on the moon. North American Rockwell, of the Los Angeles area, manufactured the spacecraft for NASA.

## 1976

★ **Spacecraft to operate on the surface of Mars**—Pasadena's Jet Propulsion Laboratory operated the *Viking* lander program in which the unmanned *Viking* spacecraft completed a 10-month journey to Mars and explored the Martian surface, providing scientific information about the planet's atmosphere and landscape. The mission began on August 20, 1975, and *Viking* landed on Mars on June 19, 1976.

## 1981

★ **The space shuttle**—*Columbia,* America's first space shuttle, made its maiden flight on April 12, 1981. Designed by Rockwell, the shuttle was constructed at the company's Palmdale facility in northern Los Angeles County. Though launched from the Kennedy Space Center, it returned to California upon landing at Edwards Air Force Base on April 14.

## 1983

★ **Spacecraft to travel beyond the planets**—Launched on March 3, 1972, the unmanned *Pioneer 10* became the first spacecraft to pass Jupiter and, in 1983, cross Pluto's orbit. TRW (Thompson Ramo Wooldridge of Los Angeles) constructed the engineering prototype of *Pioneer 10,* and the NASA Jet Propulsion Laboratory was in charge of the spacecraft's operation. Today, the NASA Research Center at California's Moffett Field receives data transmitted intermittently from *Pioneer 10.*

# "I'm a Believer"
## Religion and Spirituality

In the second decade of the 20th century, traveling evangelist and faith healer Aimee Semple McPherson attracted thousands of followers across North America. It was not until the 1920s, however, when she established a permanent home for her church in Los Angeles, that she drew legions of fans to her unique services. "Sister Aimee" had become the first female superstar evangelist.

Trading in a life on the road for a relatively settled one in Southern California, McPherson began searching for what she considered the perfect site for a grand venue to house her revival, healing, and benevolent ministries. She selected a corner lot next to Echo Park in Los Angeles with a view of the lake, but lacked the funds to purchase the land. By December 1919, almost miraculously, enough donations had flowed in to buy the acreage. Fourteen months later, sufficient funds existed to break ground and begin construction. On January 1, 1923, McPherson dedicated her Angelus Temple. With its 5,500-seat interior and revolving, illuminated cross, the structure resembled an enormous theater.

McPherson was a master at marketing religion, and she used her talent and skills to draw worshipers to the Church of the Foursquare Gospel, the Christian denomination she had conceived in 1922 during a religious epiphany. Radio, newspaper, and

Evangelist and faith healer Aimee Semple McPherson was the first woman to preach a sermon over the radio and the first to receive an FCC radio license. *Courtesy of the Security Pacific Collection/Los Angeles Public Library*

newsletter became her tools for proselytizing and for publicizing her church. Never one to pass up an opportunity for positive publicity, McPherson entered a float in Pasadena's Tournament of Roses Parade on the very day Angelus Temple was dedicated. Featuring a miniature version of the temple covered with red roses and white carnations, the float won the Grand Marshal's trophy.

McPherson brought modern jazz to the church through its Angelus Temple orchestra. Among the musicians was a teenage saxophone player named Anthony Quinn—later a well-known actor. Quinn also doubled as McPherson's onstage translator for Spanish-speaking members of the congregation.

McPherson wrote, directed, and acted in what she called her "illustrated sermons," short stage plays meant to illuminate Bible stories. She

It was not unusual for Sister Aimee to attract crowds of more than 5,000 to her Sunday evening services at Angelus Temple. *Courtesy of Teri Davis Greenberg*

believed that to grab the attention of the congregation and keep members coming back each Sunday evening, she needed to incorporate theatrical entertainment into the service. Therefore, she used modern music, props, special lighting, sound effects, costumed actors, and other accouterments of the theater.

Whether roaring down the aisle of the temple on a motorcycle as she did in her "The Green Light Is On" sermon or playing the role of a mechanic who saves the day as in "The Merry Go Round Broke Down," McPherson was ever the consummate actress and show-woman. Some Christian leaders criticized her for making the religious message take a back seat to its delivery. Members of the contemporary press referred to her as the "Barnum of religion" and the "Mary Pickford of revivalism." Others called her illustrated sermons "vaudeville of the church."

According to Sarah Comstock in *Harper's Weekly*, McPherson's Sunday evening services were the hottest ticket in town:

In this unique house of worship called Angelus Temple in the city of Los Angeles . . . Aimee Semple McPherson is staging, month after month, and even year after year, the most perennially successful show in the United States. . . . Her Sunday evening service is a complete vaudeville program, entirely new each week, brimful of surprises for the eager who are willing to battle in the throng for entrance.

McPherson's church was incorporated and registered as the International Church of the Foursquare Gospel (ICFG) on December 30, 1927. Over the decades it has grown tremendously. At the beginning of the 21st century, the church's worldwide members and adherents number more than 3.3 million worshiping in 26,139 churches and meeting places in 107 countries.

Tragically, the innovative, dedicated, driven, and often controversial McPherson didn't live long enough to witness the burgeoning fruits of her

Home of the Church of the Foursquare Gospel, Aimee Semple McPherson's Angelus Temple was built entirely through cash donations. The temple opened next to Echo Park, Los Angeles, on January 1, 1923. The same day, a miniature version of the temple appeared on a float in the Tournament of Roses Parade and won the Grand Marshal's trophy. *Courtesy of Teri Davis Greenberg*

life's labor. On September 27, 1944, Aimee Semple McPherson passed away from what was ruled an accidental overdose of sleeping pills.

## DRIVE-IN CHURCH: "WORSHIP AS YOU ARE . . . IN THE FAMILY CAR"

On Sunday, March 27, 1955, the Reverend Robert H. Schuller stepped atop the tarpaper roof of the Orange Drive-In's snack bar and began preaching to curious worshipers who sat in their cars.

Though this novel approach to proselytizing was well suited to Southern California, Schuller's fellow Reformed Church in America colleagues and many of his co-religionists found the venue completely unsuitable and undignified for a worship service. In Schuller's words: "My denomination shunned me when they heard I was preaching in a drive-in theater."

Originally, Schuller had not planned on ministering outdoors in a drive-in; financial and other circumstances led him there. The Reformed Church in America had sent the young pastor to Garden Grove, California, to establish a church, but provided him with only $500 in seed money. Unable to find an affordable hall for services, the pastor rented the Orange Drive-In for $10. He then placed an enticing advertisement in the *Orange County Register:*

Worship in the Shadows of Rising Mountains, Surrounded by Colorful Orange Groves and Tall Eucalyptus Trees . . . Storytime for the youngsters, outstanding choral singing, playground nursery for children, inspiring preaching . . . Worship as you are . . . in the family car.

Arvella Schuller, the pastor's wife, was the church's first organist, and Schuller himself carried an organ back and forth on his trailer.

Parishioner Doris Carlton, who attended the first service, remembers reading the advertisement: "I moved here in 1953, and had not found a church I felt comfortable with. When I saw an ad in the *Register* for this drive-in church service, it really intrigued me. I thought, well, it's outside, why not?"

More than 50 people attended that first drive-in service. According to Carlton, the idea of being able to worship without getting out of the car soon became a draw in itself: "It was appealing to people who didn't want to dress up for church, which is what you did in those days. Some came in their beach clothes."

By 1956, the congregation had grown enough to finance the construction of a nearby chapel, complete with stained-glass windows. To accom-

---

### *MORE FIRSTS FROM THE REVEREND ROBERT SCHULLER*

- ★ Referring to his denominational church as a "community church"
- ★ Calling a sermon a "message"
- ★ Conducting door-to-door research
- ★ Utilizing modern marketing strategies to reach religiously unaffiliated people
- ★ Providing leadership training for pastors
- ★ Televising a weekly church service

modate his sick and disabled parishioners who could not leave their cars, Schuller conducted two services each Sunday—one in the chapel and one in the drive-in sanctuary. Eventually tiring of this routine, Schuller envisioned what would become the world's first "walk-in, drive-in church." He discussed the idea with noted architect Richard Neutra, who believed that "modern architecture must act as a social force in the betterment of mankind."

Schuller sold the chapel and soon began construction on the unique Neutra-designed facility. Since 1930, the Vienna-born Neutra had enjoyed the reputation of being *the* Los Angeles architect. One architectural critic credits Neutra with creating "a modern regionalism for Southern California which combined a light metal frame with a stucco finish to create a light, effortless appearance."

When the congregation of Garden Grove Community Church dedicated its new Lewis Street facility in 1961, its members gazed upon a modern-looking church building with the parking lot capacity to accommodate drive-in worshipers as well. Five years later, the multistory Tower of Hope was built. In *Los Angeles: The Architecture of Four Ecologies*, architectural writer Reyner Banham describes Neutra's design of Schuller's one-of-a-kind church: "He achieved a notable 'first' in Internal Combustion City—a drive-in church. If there is a building that sums up, quietly and monumentally, what the peculiar automotive mania of Los Angeles is all about, Garden Grove Community Church must be the one."

As the Garden Grove congregation continued to grow, so did the need for major expansion. So in 1978, the congregation broke ground for a much larger church. Designed by architect Philip Johnson, the all-glass, 2,736-seat Crystal Cathedral was dedicated in 1980. Since that time, the spectacular structure and the Reverend Robert H. Schuller have both become known the world over via the minister's television program. His *Hour of Power*, broadcast from the Crystal Cathedral, reaches an audience of about 30 million viewers in more than 180 countries—quite a contrast from a young minister preaching from the roof of a drive-in theater's concession stand.

In 1966, against the backdrop of a slowly progressing civil rights movement and the 1965 race riots in the Watts section of Los Angeles, scholar and activist Maulana Karenga, of California State University, Long Beach, created Kwanzaa, the first African American cultural holiday.

Frustrated and disturbed by the state of African Americans' social progress, Karenga looked to African history for solutions to the problems. In his research of African cultures, Karenga saw hope for black Americans. If they were helped to reconnect with their cultural roots, Karenga believed, his people could achieve their social goals. To this end, he created Kwanzaa as a special time of year (December 26 to January 1) during which people of African ancestry could reflect on, learn from, and celebrate their common heritage. A nonreligious holiday, Kwanzaa is based on the philosophy of *Kawaida*, described by Karenga as "the constant practice of asking questions and seeking answers from African culture to the fundamental and enduring concerns of the African and human community."

Kwanzaa is actually a synthesis of various festivals celebrated by different African groups, including, but not limited to, the Zulu, Yoruba, and Ashanti peoples. At the heart of the holiday are the Seven Principles (*Nguzo Saba*), the communitarian values of unity, self-determination, collective work and responsibility, cooperative economics, purpose, creativity, and faith. Dr. Karenga conceived Kwanzaa as a time to introduce,

### ORIGIN OF THE WORD "KWANZAA"

*Kwanzaa* comes from the Swahili phrase *matunda ya kwanza*, which means "first fruits." Dr. Maulana Karenga added the third *a* to distinguish the holiday from the Swahili word.

reinforce, and cultivate these values. It is a time for gathering together, for reverence, for commemoration, for recommitment, and of course, for celebration.

At the beginning of the 21st century, more than 20 million African Americans, Africans, Caribbean and South American blacks, and members of African communities in England and Europe celebrate Kwanzaa, making it the world's fastest-growing holiday.

## MINISTERING TO THE GAY COMMUNITY: THE UFMCC

On Sunday, October 6, 1968, at 1:30 P.M., Troy D. Perry and 12 others gathered in the living room of a small, pink house in Huntington Park for a Christian worship service. While the service did not seem too different from other Christian services, the worshipers were feeling very different in this new-found congregation. They felt accepted, unashamed, and loved by God. So began the Metropolitan Community Church, the first church "to recognize the necessity of ministering to the needs of gays, lesbians, bisexuals, and transgendered persons," according to Troy Perry and Thomas Swicegood in *Don't Be Afraid Anymore*.

While the church was born in 1968, thoughts of its inception had been incubating in the mind of founder Troy Perry for years. Perry, a former fundamentalist minister, had been unceremoniously asked to leave both the Church of God and the Church of God of Prophecy when his homosexuality was discovered and deemed unacceptable by the leaders of both churches. In 1967, while Perry was stationed in Germany for the U.S. Army, a fellow soldier suggested he start his own church when he returned stateside. Perry considered the idea, but did not do anything about it at the time. Upon his discharge at the age of 27, Perry moved to the Los Angeles area. Little did he know at the time how profoundly this move to California would influence his life and, later on, the emotional and spiritual lives of thousands of gay, lesbian, bisexual, and transgendered individuals.

Three events in California finally led Perry to start his own church. First, after the breakup of a relationship, Perry tried, unsuccessfully, to kill himself. While healing from his suicide attempt, Perry began to renew his relationship with God, and he thought back to his army buddy's suggestion about starting his own church.

The second event that nudged Perry into starting a church where gay people could feel accepted was witnessing the arrest of a friend by undercover Los Angeles police at a gay bar. The friend had not done anything unlawful, but the police charged him with "lewd conduct," a term used at the time as a catch-all for "being" a homosexual.

Following this arrest, a group of gay men marched to the police station and for the first time took a public stand against the harassment and disrespect the police made them endure as a group. Perry knew the time had come to start his church when he prayed to God that night:

> Lord, you called me to preach. Now I think I've seen my niche
> in the ministry. We need a church, not a homosexual church,
> but a special church that will reach out to the lesbian and gay
> community. A church for people in trouble, and for people who
> just want to be near you. So, if you want such a church started,
> and you seem to keep telling me that you do, well then, just let
> me know when.

As Perry tells it, God answered him with "Now."

Soon after, Perry placed an advertisement in the *Advocate* announcing his new church and the time and place of the first meeting. At the initial service, Perry explained to the 12 attendees that God had told him to preach a three-pronged gospel: salvation, community, and Christian social action. Then the minister preached his first Metropolitan Community Church sermon—"Be True to You."

From that day on, the Metropolitan Community Church, now officially called the Universal Fellowship of Metropolitan Community Churches (UFMCC), began to grow and hasn't stopped.

After meeting first in Perry's living room and then in various scattered locations, the UFMCC finally consecrated its first church building on March 7, 1971. Located at the corner of 22nd and Union Streets in Los Angeles, it was the first property in the United States owned by a gay organization. In 1973, the building burned down. Undaunted by the tragedy, however, church members rebuilt the mother church. (As the church grew, 16 additional sites were intentionally burned, with three of the fires occurring in 1973.)

Today, with 300 congregations in 16 countries, UFMCC membership exceeds 44,000. The church has been featured in major magazines and newspapers around the world, as well as on *60 Minutes, Dateline, Nightline,* and various PBS presentations. On July 11, 1999, the church held a public dedication ceremony for its UFMCC World Center on Santa Monica Boulevard in West Hollywood. More than 3,000 people attended the event.

# "Cool Places"
## Entertainment and Leisure

### FIRST THEMED AMUSEMENT PARK—KNOTT'S BERRY FARM

Though Walter and Cordelia Knott did not create the boysenberry, they unwittingly turned the tiny fruit and a whole lot of fried chicken into Knott's Berry Farm—America's first themed amusement park and a famous multimillion-dollar Orange County attraction.

Rudy Boysen, the Anaheim parks superintendent, had created the boysenberry by crossing a red raspberry, a loganberry, and a blackberry. For some reason, Boysen could not keep the plants alive for more than a few days. With Boysen's permission, Buena Park berry farmer Walter Knott took Boysen's six plants and nursed them back to life.

By the early 1930s, Knott was selling "boysenberry" plants to customers who stopped by the tea room/berry stand/nursery that he and his wife, Cordelia, had built on their Buena Park land in 1928. When the Great Depression hit, Cordelia began making and selling boysenberry jams and jellies to help support their family of six. Next, she sold boysenberry pies along with biscuits and sandwiches. Then, one night in June 1934, she served eight fried-chicken dinners (on her wedding china) to visitors for 65 cents a plate. Word spread quickly about her delicious chicken dinners and boysenberry pie, and soon Cordelia Knott found herself in the restaurant business.

In 1911, newlyweds Walter and Cordelia Knott posed for their wedding portrait. *Courtesy of KNOTT'S BERRY FARM: © 2000 Knott's Berry Farm*

By 1940, the restaurant was serving between 1,500 and 4,000 dinners on Sunday nights, forcing patrons to wait in extremely long lines. Wanting to keep his customers satisfied, Walter Knott devised a plan to entertain (and distract) them while they waited. Having had a lifelong interest in the Old West, he decided to transform his berry farm into a Western-themed attraction named Knott's Berry Place.

First, he relocated the Old Trails Hotel from Prescott, Arizona, to the farm and installed "The Covered Wagon Show" in the hotel lobby. The hotel and the wagon show (actually a diorama depicting his ancestors' journey west) were the core of the park's first themed area—Ghost Town. Knott, who as a young man had worked in the mines in the town of Calico, returned to the town, bought some of its buildings, and relocated them to his Ghost Town. Seven years later, Knott officially renamed his park Knott's Berry Farm.

In the 1950s, the Calico Saloon, Calico Railroad (an actual Denver & Rio Grande narrow-gauge train), and Bird Cage Theatre were added to Ghost Town. The 1960s brought the Calico Mine Ride, an exact replica of

Knott's Berry Farm, "America's First Themed Amusement Park," started out in 1928 as a tea-room, berry stand, and nursery named Knott's Berry Place. *Courtesy of KNOTT'S BERRY FARM: ©2000 Knott's Berry Farm*

Philadelphia's Independence Hall, the Calico Mining Company ride (later renamed the Timber Mountain Log Ride), and the debut of the park's second themed area—Fiesta Village. In 1968, the Knott family enclosed the park and charged admission for the first time.

By the 1970s, the hybrid "themed-amusement park" had added the John Wayne Theatre (now the Chevrolet/Geo Good Time Theatre), initiated its Knott's Scary Farm Halloween Haunt (the world's first amusement-park Halloween promotion), and added the park's third themed area—the Roaring '20s—which included Corkscrew (the first 360-degree roller coaster in the world), Knott's Bear-y Tales, and the 20-story Sky Jump and Sky Cabin. Montezooma's Revenge, the park's second roller coaster (which can travel from 0 to 55 miles per hour in five seconds) debuted in Fiesta Village.

With the opening of six-acre Camp Snoopy (the first area of any amusement or theme park designed solely for children under the age of 12) in the 1980s, the "Peanuts" characters became Knott's staples. The '80s also saw the opening of the Pacific Pavilion in the Roaring '20s section, Kingdom of the Dinosaurs (which replaced Knott's Bear-y Tales), and Bigfoot Rapids in the Knott's Wild Water Wilderness area.

Hard Boiled Hat for use b
the year following the o
designed and manufacture
reasonably lightweight hat
its application was limited.
three-rib, heat-resistant fibe
by thermoplastic hats. Bull
thermoplastic into a mold t

Due to a request from th
for a hard hat with the pro
pany ushered in a new er
today's standard yellow po
nonslip, ratchet-suspensior
ment. In addition, the eas
with an ultraviolet inhibito

Other Bullard innovatio
"Advent" and "Vector" mo
ed against impact not only t
and back.

machine. Fey
also a partner
the machines
time to creati
man named
coin-operated
Market Stree
Historical La

In 1899, Fe
he named th
machines ma
and renamed
and other fr
the first reel
clubs, and h
around the
10 symbols
stopped one
bols possibl
lined up to
jackpot, a b
became star

The Libe
made of cas
of the Liber
metal feet.

Fey mac
try. Unwill
it he made
clubs, and
from one of
would chan
Chicago-ba
saloons an
Bell" slot r

aboard to
land, he h
Soon L
Francisco
Street wh
that the m
with then
pants that
When a m
them from
was so hap
talking the
Seeing t
had to the
more. The
ers in New
Levi and
clientele.
Company,
tial for the
as a retaile
local store
By this t
law, Willia
wholesale
Francisco.
In 1866, co
headquarte
Business
from one of
would char
Levi, had a
working. D

If you wo
at http://c

Skelet
c/o Th
1104 N
Los An
You ca
Pacific

The Los A
shop. The firs
made for its
employees p
their own. In
dents led to c
uted credit ca
ing message "
As word of
ager Marilyn
and more pho
mer intern, Le
shirts took ov
the Closet.
Soon "Skele
Bones"—and
gifts. No longe
cated to the se
70 murder- an

**OTHER DISNEY THEM**

★ Walt Disney World Resort near Orlando,
theme parks: The Magic Kingdom (1
"Experimental Prototype Community of
Studios (1989); and Disney's Animal Kin
★ Tokyo Disneyland (1983)
★ Disneyland Paris (1992)

Disneyland comprised Main Street,
hood home of Marceline, Missouri
Fantasyland, and Tomorrowland.
Country/Critter Country, and Mickey'
One dollar bought entrance into the pa
ning from 10 cents to 35 cents each.
months after opening, Disneyland ha
The following month, ticket books wer
rides and attractions (A for the cheape
1956, D tickets were added, and in 195
(E tickets procured admission to the m

When Walt was in his mid-60s, he
Animatronics" to produce mannequi
wishing to spend his own money test
procured a contract with the State of
1964 World's Fair in New York. The
Lincoln"—proved the hit of the fair
Street, U.S.A., in Disneyland Park.
Disneyland attractions have incorpor
to bring Walt's dream of happiness a
of Disneyland guests.

Before the year 2000, Knott's Berry Farm had replaced Corkscrew with
Boomerang, Ghost Town had celebrated its 50th anniversary, the two-acre
Indian Trails and Knott's Mystery Lodge had debuted, the park had celebrated its 75th anniversary, and the Roaring '20s area had been transformed into The Boardwalk, with the first outdoor dual steel racing coaster—Windjammer—as its main attraction. In addition, five other new
attractions had made their first appearances: Edison International Electric
Nights, Supreme Scream (the world's tallest descending thrill ride),
Woodstock's Airmail (a kid-size version of Supreme Scream), a completely renovated version of Walter Knott's Independence Hall, and the 4,533-
foot-long, 118-foot-high GhostRiders roller coaster (the West's longest
wooden coaster).

In 1998, after having owned the park since its 1920 inception as a berry
stand, the Knott family sold it to Cedar Fair LP. From its original 20 acres,
Knott's Berry Farm now occupies 150 acres and ranks as the nation's 12th-
most-visited themed amusement park. For up-to-date visitor information,
check out the park's Web site, www.knotts.com.

### To Visit: Knott's Berry Farm

Knott's Berry Farm
8039 Beach Boulevard
Buena Park, CA 90620
714-220-5200
Hours: Vary; call to verify.
Admission charged.

## FIRST DISNEY THEME PARK—DISNEYLAND

*"I think what I want Disneyland to be most of all is a happy place, a
place where adults and children can experience together some of the
wonders of life, of adventure, and feel better because of it."*

Walter Elias "Walt" Disney

so they could learn from others' mista
ground for the company's first Magic
Anaheim. Excavation began the follow

On July 17, 1955, Disneyland Park
More than 28,000 people attended t
watched it on ABC television. Walt de

To all who come to this happy pl
your land. Here age relives fond
youth may savor the challenge a
Disneyland is dedicated to the i
facts that have created America
source of joy and inspiration to

thinking
Soon th
girls" an
concept
go-go da

Amon
years we
Hendrix,
Night, Bl
as the ho
and went

Thoug
reopened
Following
well as up

The Wl
the officia
States Pos
Peace Syn

 **To Vis**

The W
8901 S
West H
310-65.
www.v

**THE CORO**

Located tw
the most bi
nation's firs

outside
Louisv
in the S
there, h

Whe
Strauss
in the l
per shi
bringin
ers, he
Coast b
Francis

Though
subsequent
jeans are th
1800s. 501 j
Co." Since
as waist o
"jeans." Fir
as jeans.

**THREE-RE**

Risk-takin
mining ca
Barbary C
and other

These
were mon
mostly in
1870 requ
and drink
he could

It wasn
*when* they
ing mach
stood the
owners
changed.

In 189
machine
machine
immigra
1885, cre
Coast b
Francis

his time and energy to
with coming up with th
for "Save Our Saucepans

Edwin Cox turned his
creating and selling anotl
product is still a staple i

**THE HARD HAT: KEEPIN**

Little more than 50 years
ment for American worl
forms, in oil fields, or in
and others who visited jo
a San Franciscan named
have been saved and inj

Edward D. Bullard, w
the 1890s, founded a n
Selling carbide lamps an
Bullard observed that th
bies with small, hard, sh
tection from falling objec

When E. W. Bullard, E
he began working on the
Using his "doughboy" he
ating the world's first c
device. Because the man
layers of glued canvas, B
In 1919, he patented the b
and sold it to the Phelps
mining companies seekir

In the early 1930s, bas
tective-equipment busir
Golden Gate Bridge con

Now, with a working electric guitar in hand, Beauchamp asked his friend and former National production engineer Adolph "Rick" Rickenbacker to help him start a company to produce it. Rickenbacker agreed to invest the necessary capital to begin manufacturing the new electric instrument. The partners initially named their company the Ro-Pat-In Corporation, but soon changed the name to the Electro String Instrument Corporation. Rickenbacker was president, and Beauchamp was secretary-treasurer.

Rickenbacker and Beauchamp rented a shop at 6071 South Western Avenue in Los Angeles (next to Rickenbacker's tool and die plant) to produce what became known as the Rickenbacker model A-22 laptop steel electric, or the "Electro Hawaiian." From the wooden prototype, the company began production of the cast-aluminum Frying Pan in 1932, just after Beauchamp filed his first patent application on the guitar. The technology involved in the Frying Pan's electromagnetic pickup has changed little since then.

Two years after filing for his first patent, Beauchamp filed a revised application. When two different patent examiners expressed their doubt over the guitar's operational ability, Rickenbacker sent a group of guitarists to Washington, D.C., to prove that the electric guitar was functional. Finally, in 1937, the U.S. Patent Office issued a patent for the guitar to Beauchamp.

After overcoming some obstacles that impeded initial sales of the guitar—the slow-moving patent office, the Great Depression, musicians' reluctance to accept electric instruments—the Frying Pan did, in fact, sell well thanks to the Hawaiian-music craze of the 1930s.

Though the Electro String Instrument Corporation was best known in the '30s for its electric laptop steel guitars, it went on to develop and manufacture other types of steel guitars, including a Bakelite plastic model, Spanish (standard) models, a couple of electric archtop models, and a 1935 Bakelite Spanish guitar that set a trend for all solid-body guitars that followed. The company also produced amplifiers, some of which ended up in Leo Fender's radio repair shop in Fullerton. (Fender, later famous for mass-producing the Telecaster and Stratocaster electric guitars, earned the nickname "the Henry Ford of the electric guitar.")

As his health began to deteriorate, Beauchamp sold his interest in the company to Rickenbacker's bookkeeper in 1940. Shortly thereafter, Beauchamp died of a heart attack. Rickenbacker continued to produce electric instruments until 1953, when he sold the company to Francis C. ("F. C.") Hall, who owned an electronics parts distribution company known as Radio-Tel (later the distributing arm for Rickenbacker guitars). Before buying Electro String, Hall had been Fender's national distributor of steel guitar and amplifier sets. He gave up selling Fender products when given the opportunity to own the company that had produced the first viable electric guitar.

Hall, realizing that the market was moving away from "lap" steels and toward electric standard guitars, concentrated production on the latter. Under Hall's leadership, Electro String introduced the novel "neck-through-body" construction design, and in 1958, a hollow-body six-string model.

The company's best public relations coup came in the early 1960s when the Beatles were seen worldwide playing several Rickenbacker models. According to the company, the Beatles "created unprecedented international interest in Rickenbackers." By the mid-1960s, demand for Rickenbackers had resulted in about a six-month production backup at the

## The Zamboni in Art, Film, and Music

In January 1980, celebrated cartoonist Charles Schulz introduced the Zamboni to readers of his famous "Peanuts" comic strip and went on to include the machine in 44 of his cartoons. In fact, Snoopy and Woodstock are two of the most famous Zamboni drivers. (Woodstock drives the Zamboni around his frozen birdbath to prepare it for ice skating.)

★ *EDtv,* starring Matthew McConaughey, featured the character of Ed driving a Zamboni around the ice to the cheers of hockey fans.

★ "The Zamboni Song" appears on The Gear Daddies' CD titled *Billy's Live Bait* as a hidden track (#10).

★ In the 1980s, a Vancouver-based duo named the Zamboni Drivers was a mainstay on the British Columbia music scene.

## FOAM SURFBOARDS: SURFING'S SECOND WAVE

The evolution of the surfboard from wood to foam represented a major breakthrough in surfing. Developed over a period of several years by a number of Southern California surfers, the lighter-weight boards introduced women, children, and 90-pound weaklings to a sport once ruled by men who could carry a 100-to-150-pound megaboard from the car to the ocean. Because the new boards were also easier to manufacture, the number produced increased dramatically beginning in the 1950s. As a result, the sport that had once been considered the domain of beach bums and beatniks went mainstream.

Polyurethane foam, fiberglass, and resin—the three main components of modern surfboards—resulted from World War II military research, and the first surfers to experiment with the new materials were Preston "Pete" Peterson, Brant Goldsworthy, and Ted Thal of Los Angeles. In June 1946, with the help of Goldsworthy and Thal, Peterson became the first person to build a fiberglass surfboard. Peterson's board was made of two hollow, molded halves connected with a redwood stringer for support down the

These Vietnam-era Marines competed in a 1966 surfing contest using foam-and-fiberglass surfboards. *Courtesy of the National Archives, Still Pictures Branch*

middle, and Peterson sealed the seam with fiberglass tape. Unlike its wooden predecessors, the fiberglass board was not opaque—you could see light through it.

Bob Simmons is considered the "father of the modern surfboard" and is best known for experimenting with radical board design. In 1947–48, he developed the first production-line surfboard with an expanded polystyrene (foam) core, balsa wood rails, and a plywood deck. Among his other creations were the Sandwich Board (1949), sealed plywood over a Styrofoam core; the Spoon Board (1949), 10 feet of solid balsa wood with a full belly, kicked-up nose, thin rails, and a fiberglass-and-foiled-wood fin; and a double-slotted board designed to improve paddling. Simmons tested his first boards at Malibu or Palos Verdes Cove, set up a surf shop in Santa Monica, later closed that shop and moved his operation to his family's Norwalk ranch, then moved to Imperial Beach in San Diego County. By 1950, he had stopped producing boards.

Joe Quigg, who worked with Simmons in Santa Monica, was a surfboard innovator in his own right. His lightweight, resin-sealed board made of balsa wood and fiberglass, first called the Easy Rider and later the Malibu Board (1947), dominated the surf scene of the 1950s. Other Quigg boards included the Pintail #1 (1947), the Grey Ghost (1947), the Pintail #2 (1948), the Nose Rider (1949), and a fifth pintail board (1951) made of fiberglass-covered light balsa. According to Quigg, his motive in board design "was to make stuff that was happy, more fun."

In 1955, surfing legend Lorrin "Whitey" Harrison of Capistrano Beach became the first person to build a board out of polyurethane foam, but it was Dave Sweet who first made commercial polyurethane foam surfboards (1956) at his Santa Monica shop. Financed by Cliff Robertson, who starred in the film *Gidget* with Sally Field, Sweet's surfboard business was the "first sustained effort in developing polyurethane foam boards," according to fellow manufacturing pioneer Gordon Clark.

Hobart "Hobie" Alter, who grew up in Ontario, California, began making surfboards as a teenager in his father's Laguna Beach garage during the summer of 1950. He ended up making 99 balsa boards in the garage before setting up shop in Dana Point in 1954. When high-quality balsa became difficult to find, Alter switched to polyurethane foam for his surfboards. After many unsuccessful attempts to mold the material, Alter asked his friend Gordon "Grubby" Clark to become his glasser and cover the board blanks with fiberglass. Working together, the two produced the first polyurethane foam–and-fiberglass board in June 1958. Soon Alter and Clark established a shop in Laguna Canyon where they developed a process of high-pressure molding to make the boards more stable. The ability to control the density of the foam changed surfboard manufacturing for good.

Though the surfboard-manufacturing community was close-knit, it was also highly competitive. So Alter and Clark decided on an amicable split in which Clark would make board blanks (Clark Foam, founded 1961) and Alter would remain a board designer, shaper, and marketer. The decision proved profitable for both men.

Alter's light, fast, responsive boards outperformed the competition, and soon everyone wanted a Hobie board. Today the company's popularity continues, and its Web site declares: "Hobie Alter. He started out shaping surfboards; he ended up shaping a culture."

## THE JACUZZI: FROM FAMILY NAME TO TRADEMARK

Throw the Jacuzzi into the same pool as Kleenex tissues, Band-Aid bandages, and Post-it notes, because just like the other brand names, *Jacuzzi* has become a generic term for its product type—the whirlpool spa.

The seven Jacuzzi brothers immigrated to the United States from Italy in 1907 and settled in California. During World War I, they established a machine shop and built airplane propellers for the United States Air Service. They also produced airplanes for a few years following the war.

---

### A JACUZZI AVIATION FIRST

After World War I ended, the Jacuzzi brothers ventured into airplane manufacturing and created the first enclosed-cabin, high-wing monoplane. A tragic plane crash that killed several people, including a Jacuzzi relative, led the brothers to quit the airplane business in 1921.

---

With California's farmers requiring a constant water supply, the Jacuzzi brothers seized the opportunity to enter the agricultural-pump industry. Using their combined knowledge of hydraulics, they created the first Jacuzzi pump.

In the post–World War II years, when the second generation of Jacuzzis joined the company, a family crisis arose that would, ironically, make Jacuzzi a household name in years to come. A cousin stricken with rheumatoid arthritis required daily hot hydrotherapy. To help their ailing relative, the members of the Jacuzzi engineering team made some changes to one of the company's pumps, adapting it for home use. This portable whirlpool pump, patented in 1954, later underwent some significant modifications, including the addition of water jets that utilized an air-injection system. When the J-300 portable pump was introduced in 1956, it could turn any tub into a therapeutic bath as it produced a soothing, swirling mixture of water and air bubbles. The J-300, used primarily in hospitals and doctors' offices, proved to be the foundation of a multimillion-dollar business for the Jacuzzi family.

The third generation of the family included the man responsible for launching an entire industry. Roy Jacuzzi, born in 1944, had studied industrial design before joining the family business. In the late 1960s, young Roy took note of the health-and-leisure craze beginning to sweep the country, with California leading the way. What better way to relax after a hard workout than with a soak in a whirlpool? Seeing the potential for a spin-off Jacuzzi product, Roy developed the idea of a self-contained whirlpool bath with built-in jets.

In 1968, when Roy sold his first home whirlpool bath at a California county fair, the elder Jacuzzis considered him a bit odd. Yet they started a new division of the company—Whirlpool Bath—and put Roy in charge. Soon the home whirlpool became one of the company's most profitable products. Dubbed the Roman Bath, it was considered by Jacuzzi to be the successor to the traditional non-whirlpool tub. But it quickly became obvious that the typical American could not afford the luxury product.

In 1970 Jacuzzi introduced a larger home whirlpool, and America's first spa debuted the same year. The fiberglass-molded whirlpool tub, which could hold several people at one time, was designed with built-in filtration and heating systems to keep the water clean and warm. Americans went crazy over the newest Jacuzzi, and a new industry was born.

Jacuzzi (owned by British Hanson PLC) is headquartered in Walnut Creek, but also has manufacturing and marketing divisions worldwide. The company holds the first patent on the whirlpool bath as well as 250 additional patents.

## NOTES ON CHAPTER TITLES

**Chapter 1** • **"Reelin' in the Years"**
Songwriters: Walter Becker and Donald Fagen
Performers: Steely Dan; formed in Los Angeles, 1972

**Chapter 2** • **"I Get Around"**
Songwriter: Brian Wilson
Performers: Beach Boys; formed in Hawthorne, California, 1961

**Chapter 3** • **"Show and Tell"**
Songwriter: Jerry Fuller, moved to Los Angeles from Texas when he was 21; still lives in Southern California
Performer:   Al Wilson, moved to San Bernardino from Mississippi as a teenager and after two years in the Navy, moved to Los Angeles

**Chapter 4** • **"Weird Science"**
Songwriter: Danny Elfman (raised in Los Angeles)
Performers: Oingo Boingo; formed in Los Angeles, 1979

**Chapter 5** • **"Fun Fun Fun"**
Songwriters: Brian Wilson and Mike Love
Performers: Beach Boys (see "I Get Around" notes)

**Chapter 6** • **"Eat It"**
Songwriter and Performer: "Weird" Al Yankovic, born Alfred Matthew Yankovic, Lynwood, California, 1959; graduated Lynwood High School, 1976, as valedictorian; graduated Cal Poly San Luis Obispo, 1980

**Chapter 7** • **"Up, Up and Away"**
Songwriter: Jimmy Webb, moved to California in 1964 from Oklahoma; attended San Bernardino Valley College as music major; moved to Los Angeles area
Performers: Fifth Dimension; formed 1965 in Los Angeles as Versatiles and changed name per producer Johnny Rivers in 1966

**Chapter 8** • **"I'm a Believer"**
Songwriter: Neil Diamond, moved to Los Angeles in 1968, bought beach house in Malibu in 1970s
Performers: Monkees, created 1965 in Los Angeles as a television series band (all were musicians); disbanded in 1969

**Chapter 9** • **"Cool Places"**
Songwriters: Ron and Russell Mael
Performers: Sparks, formed in Los Angeles, 1970

**Chapter 10** • **"For What It's Worth"**
Songwriter: Stephen Stills
Performers: Buffalo Springfield, formed in Los Angeles, 1966 (literally on Sunset during a traffic jam)

## SUGGESTED READINGS

Cao, Lan, and Himilce Novas. *Everything You Need to Know About Asian-American History*. New York: Penguin Books, 1996.

Epstein, Daniel Mark. *Sister Aimee: The Life of Aimee Semple McPherson*. San Diego: Harcourt, Brace, 1993.

Freeman, Allyn, and Bob Golden. *Why Didn't I Think of That?: Bizarre Origins of Ingenious Inventions We Couldn't Live Without*. New York: John Wiley & Sons, 1997.

Kahn, Edgar M. *Cable Car Days in San Francisco*. Stanford, Calif.: Stanford University Press, 1940.

Lavigne, Yves. *Hells Angels: Into the Abyss*. New York: HarperCollins, 1996.

Love, John F. *McDonald's: Behind the Arches*. New York: Bantam Books, 1986.

Perry, Troy D., with Thomas L. P. Swicegood. *Don't Be Afraid Anymore*. New York: St. Martin's Press, 1990.

Schoneberger, William A. *California Wings: A History of Aviation in the Golden State*. Woodland Hills, Calif.: Windsor Publications, 1984.

Thompson, Hunter S. *Hell's Angels: The Strange and Terrible Saga of the Outlaw Motorcycle Gangs*. New York: Ballantine Books, 1966.

Van Steenwyk, Elizabeth. *Levi Strauss: The Blue Jeans Man*. New York: Walker, 1988.

DEDICATED TO

*The memory of my grandfather, vaSekuru Murehwa, who exemplified excellence in all his endeavours.*

# CONTENTS

# ACKNOWLEDGMENTS

Immense gratitude to my son, Ruvheneko, who conceived the idea of this book and whose life inspired it.

My sincere thanks to my wife and best friend, Tembi, for her massive role in the upbringing of our son and for giving me the time, space and support to write.

To Kumud Bawa, thank you for your enthusiasm, encouragement, and review of the first few chapters of the draft.

And to the editorial team at PaperTrue, thank you so much for your contribution and invaluable feedback.

## ABOUT THE AUTHOR

Chris Chinaire was born in Harare, Zimbabwe, and came to
London, England with his wife, Tembi, and their one-year-old
son, Ruvheneko, in 1999.
He is a business intelligence and data management professional
and has worked in the finance, healthcare and legal sectors.
Chris grew up with five brothers in the Highfields suburb of
Harare (officially Salisbury until 1982) during the era of white
minority rule in the country.
He enjoys playing chess, watching football and writing on issues
closest to his heart.

chris.chinaire@ppkinfo.co.uk

# WHY I HAVE WRITTEN THIS BOOK

I had no intention of writing about a topic so dear to my heart, but my son caught me off guard when he suggested, just before turning 20, that I write a book about how he was raised. Apparently, he thought that the task had been done and dusted.

Wondering what he had in mind, I enquired, "Who is the target audience? Your friends?"

"No. Not my friends. I thought you would write it for parents."

I was taken aback. Up until then, I'd suspected he thought he could have had a better crack at fatherhood than I did. After a heated encounter in his early teens, I caught him writing a few pages on what fatherhood should look like.

And he didn't inspire much confidence when a girl in his Year 8 class presented him a perfect opportunity. A family friend overheard her daughter tell my son, "I wish your dad was my dad."

She missed her father who had recently left home after separating from her mother.

My son was quick to state, "If my dad was your dad, you would do maths during summer holidays!"

"I wouldn't."

"Yeah, you would," he declared from experience.

I hoped I hadn't given him the impression that parenting him was the execution of a well-thought-out plan. Instead, it largely entailed responding to his evolving needs. So, his temperament was in the driving seat, and my love for him and evolving wisdom provided the sign posts.

My son was born in Harare, Zimbabwe, and arrived in London two months after his first birthday. His battle for life could have been fought anywhere, each place presenting different dynamics. Raising him in London was incomparable to doing so anywhere else. The global city, adopted home to almost every race and nationality, exposed him to every imaginable culture.

His mother came to join the NHS, and I was drawn to the vast IT industry. We thought the work and life experience would be priceless. Nothing prepared us for the challenges of simultaneously raising a black boy in Greater London.

I spent more time with him in his formative years than his mother, as NHS duty called. We didn't realise the price he paid for this until one evening, aged six, he confronted her, "Where are you going?"

"Work."

"Work, work, work. You're always going to work! Just tell your boss you quit!"

It was fortunate that at least one of us didn't do shift work. It enabled me to play a bigger parenting role than I would have under different circumstances.

No book could ever hold a complete account of how he was raised; contrary to his belief, the task will never be complete. This book is a selection of the major factors I responded to.

# ONE: INTRODUCTION

G oing back in time and piecing together the highs and lows of fatherhood was not too difficult. Every event had been mentally catalogued and internally indexed by place, emotion, sound, smell, and countless other attributes.

The smell of dust could trigger a replay of a three-legged race at a Year 2 sports day that my son and his friend, Rio, had effortlessly won. I can still feel the discomfort of getting excited for him while aiding a helpless mother console one of his less agile friends.

How fast time has flown! Nineteen years packed with unforgettable firsts and lasts. I had narrowed down fatherhood to three primary roles: provider, protector, and teacher. But it turned out there were many more hats to wear.

I was a permanent presence in his corner of life's boxing ring. Much as I would have liked to fight for him and even shield him, only he could engage in the battle for his life. Experience enabled me to provide timely and honest feedback, some of which he took on board. But at times it took a knockdown for him to see sense.

I was also the relay race forerunner who passed the baton on to release him to run his own race. Most of our disagreements turned out to be centred on the timing of the passing of the baton. He thought he was ready to run even before he could walk.

## Truth Buffets

My son grew up in the age of truth buffets, a time when the majority only consumed what was palatable to their tastes. Every other person had become adept at directing the spotlight on snippets of the truth while keeping the rest in the dark. So, half-truths usually eclipsed the whole truth.

Facts played second fiddle to what the influential either endorsed or wanted to believe. Information pyramids could be overturned to publish insights drawn from data yet to be gathered.

Before elections, truth was what the electorate expected, and immediately afterwards it changed to what the elected wanted the electorate to believe.

Historical commentary couldn't be taken for granted. The colonial era was at times depicted as a crusade of mercy, while Africa was generally portrayed as a place where time stood still to watch the rest of the world progress.

Conflicting conclusions could be drawn from the same facts. For instance, there were different schools of thought on why a disproportionately high number of black boys in England and Wales were (and still are) in prison.

The dilemma was where and when to start setting the record

straight. We were already playing catch-up to a misinformation machinery that had had quite a head start.

Although only he could tell his own story with any credibility, there was no shortage of volunteers eager to teach him who he was. But he soon learned that even the animal kingdom narrated its own story.

## Law of the jungle

Africa's wildlife programmes intrigued him from the very first time we watched one together. He found the animal kingdom transparent, with no hidden agendas, except in long grass or darkness when predators were on the prowl. It introduced him to the law of the jungle – survival of the fittest.

Every type of animal is uniquely equipped to perfect the art of survival. Living to see another day is only one part of the story. The complete picture includes the flourishing of every kind, with every member playing a significant part.

He noticed the jungle was in constant flux and renewal, forever pruning itself of vulnerabilities. So, lagging behind its pace of change rarely went unpunished.

Boundaries, physical and virtual, overlapped, with every type of animal observing its own. Power was the currency of choice to settle territorial disputes.

He came to understand that, contrary to history, the law of the jungle established the world order and the food chain hierarchy. And Africa was one of the many hunting grounds that had been secured by military might.

While animal conservation and wildlife programme makers adopted a policy of non-interference, the same courtesy was not extended to the custodians of the continent's wildlife, who were forced to follow in the footsteps of Europe in terms of culture, language, and religion. It was tantamount to training the highly social African wild dogs to adopt the solitary lifestyle of foxes.

He concluded that the world order wasn't as it should be largely because Africa had been diverted off its natural course.

### Sieving facts

We instilled in him the notion that he was not obliged to take anything at face value and urged him to constantly sieve details for truth. There was no room for indifference.

A one-dimensional view of anything can distort the truth. The onus was, therefore, on him to look for all the angles.

David Livingstone's exploration of Africa was a good case in point. History has hardly mentioned the African hospitality without which Livingstone wouldn't have been able to venture into the unknown. He was welcomed as a guest and given guides to significant sites such as the Mosi-oa-Tunya, which he renamed the Victoria Falls.

Also understated was the people's ability to quickly learn foreign languages. But this unsung skill opened channels of communication, facilitated negotiations and enabled Livingstone to teach.

He thought that this explained why most of Africa is multilingual. Most people are fluent in at least two African languages and one European language. This compelled him to question what is ordinarily taken on face value.

Open days at school and college revealed that my son was actively engaged in his classes. At a parents' evening at college, a teacher's initial remarks were "Your son is different from most students. He won't accept anything that hasn't been explained to his satisfaction. I prepare lessons with him in mind. He is one of my favourite students."

Though it didn't always translate into improved grades, we were pleased with his preparedness to probe.

# TWO: SELF-PERCEPTION

It was logical to us that our son was going to view the world through the same lens with which he saw himself. So, we helped him paint as accurate a portrait of himself in his mind as possible, keeping our role peripheral to minimise the risk of getting in the way of the artist in him.

That turned out to be the easy part. The bigger challenge was to prevent vandalisation. Mental graffiti was neither easy to spot nor straightforward to clean up.

### Self-portrayal

My son's self-portrayal began at infancy. He was born with a mandate to continually progress, setting the stage for the collision of contrary perceptions.

Every cry for attention rang with the expectation of a prompt response and immediate understanding of the need. So, quite early on, he became accustomed to frustration, as he watched us use a process of trial and error to identify the source of his discomforts. It set him off on a learning journey to become a part of the solution to his own needs.

He was bemused by celebrations of what we considered significant milestones. To him, each was only a gateway to the next phase. By the time he had mastered the strength and balance to stand, his focus had already shifted to walking. It was always the next stage that lured him.

Electronic toys held his attention only for so long. It was "game over" immediately after all the functions on the remote control had been explored. The next challenge was to look into the inner workings of each toy. And so he dismantled every toy to find this out, intending to put it back together after his investigations. But re-assembling turned out to be more of a challenge. He had to work out the purpose of every part.

Early on, he understood he was one of a kind and purposefully unique. How he felt about himself was established by the time he could distinguish the different shades of *black*. Our large bathroom mirror showed that he and I were a dark chocolate brown, in contrast to his mother's honey brown shade.

### Blacks vs whites friendly

By the time he started school in West London, I thought he was comfortable with who he was – a notion that was confirmed one morning on the train to work when he was six.

I sat next to the mother of a girl in his class, Dee. In the middle of a polite conversation, she suddenly stopped as if she had remembered something important. She clicked her fingers, smiled widely and declared, "You know, I really like your son."

She drew closer to me, lowered her voice and added, "Dee told me everyone was shocked when he organised a break-time football match between black and white boys".

It was the first time I had heard about it. So, I probed for more information.

"It happened last week. You know, perhaps because your son is a man, he has pride in who he is. Much as I have tried to tell Dee she is beautiful, she wishes she had blue eyes and blond hair. I really like your boy!"

It seemed she had more intel on my son than I did. My daily after-school probe was not yielding vital information. Perhaps he thought the one-word answer, "fine", adequately encapsulated the happenings of the day. I resolved to change tact.

I half-expected a denial when at the end of the day I asked him, from an informed position, "Did you have a break-time football match pitting the black boys against the white boys last week?"

Surprise briefly flashed on his face before he enquired, "How did you know?"

Making the most of the rare moment, I trumpeted, "I have my sources."

"When was the match?" I continued to probe.

"Last Wednesday."

"Why did you pit black boys against whites?"

"We had no uniforms. So, I suggested we take our shirts off and use our skin colours instead."

"Did it work?"

"Yeah."

"How did the match go?"

With a happy smile, he reported, "We hammered them, Dad. We hammered them."

I must confess, in that moment of glee, it didn't once cross my mind to wonder how I would have responded had a white boy hatched this novel idea.

# THREE: EDUCATION

## Transition to primary school

The last few weeks at nursery school seemed to drag on forever for him. He was so looking forward to going to the *big school* that we concluded he was ready to be stretched. He had outgrown all the toys and learned almost everything there was to learn. There was just one last lesson to grasp before departing – the art of saying goodbye.

His first serious farewell took much longer than we had anticipated. There were tears, his teacher's and his, followed by a vow to keep in touch. So, for a month and a half after his departure, we passed by his old nursery school about once a week.

His primary school was among the best in the area. My wife and I loved everything about it. But it turned out to be very different from the picture he had in his mind. There was a distinct demarcation between lessons and playtime, and he thought there was too little of the latter. So, he had to curb the vast amount of energy within just to avoid getting into trouble. And as if that wasn't bad enough, he could no longer leave it all behind after school. There was homework to be considered, in the form of yet another encroachment on his playtime. So, from the outset, our different perceptions of school put us on opposite sides of the fence.

## Doing the minimum

His insatiable thirst for knowledge meant he didn't need convincing that education was a necessity. We were, however, at odds about how we viewed the structured, regimented ways of learning in the earliest years. He often resorted to doing the absolute minimum required to maintain the peace at home. When he eventually found joy in his school work, he could not immediately undo every poor habit that had taken deep roots.

He seemed to have gone into auto pilot when his Year 5 class was tasked with writing a minimum of 99 words about what they had each done during the spring holidays. His teacher had made it clear that she was going to fail any essay that had less than the minimum required word count.

She later told us that he had diligently written his holiday account, occasionally pausing to count the words to ensure he was on track. He had only handed it in after convincing himself he had done what was required.

"How many words did you write?" the teacher asked.

"99."

"Exactly 99?"

"Yeah."

Upon counting in his presence, the teacher found he had 98 words.

"Damn! I'm one short."

It turned out to be a harsh lesson about the risk of aiming to just avoid failure. It was a pivotal moment for him as he decided to start aiming higher. Intending to do well was safer grounds. Homework became less of a battle ground as his work ethic improved.

## Maths

At first, he resented having to do Maths during his holidays until it dawned on him that how he felt made little difference to the task at hand. He couldn't see how any of the theorems could apply to the life he imagined he would lead beyond his school days. He had concluded that Maths was about providing answers to problems he was unlikely to face in the future.

He was therefore surprised that I was not impressed when he resorted to pulling the answers out of his retentive mind, without applying the related logic. It wasn't immediately clear to him why there was more value in the journey to every answer than the answer itself.

There was no quick way to illustrate that Maths was going to teach him how to think and to correctly apply logic. It was only fortunate that we had time on our hands. High-profile violent incidents in the city helped him understand that black boys do not have the liberty to take off their thinking caps, not even during school holidays.

The more he stayed on course, the more open his mind became. In time, he removed Maths from the list of hated subjects. Though it didn't quite become a favourite, he gained a better understanding of not only the principles, but also the wider application of logic.

## Sex education

He was almost three when I first realised that I should have started the basics of sex education earlier. We were on our way home from the nursery school when a small dog quickly ran past us, prompting him to point out, "That's a girl dog."

Thinking he already knew the dog from the neighbourhood, I asked, "How do you know?"

"Dad, I know the difference between boys and girls."

Though it wasn't the conversation I thought we were having, we just had to proceed once we were on the road.

"What's the difference?"

"Girls have no privates."

I took it as a cue to set the record straight, that girls do have privates, only a different kind. They do not hang down like boys' privates. Theirs are concealed behind protective layers. Over time, we spoke about where babies come from, where he came from, and the essence of sex.

He was fourteen when we revisited the subject more seriously. I didn't know what to expect when his high school notified us that his class was going to have a sex education lesson the following day. It was the first thing I brought up when I got home from work the next day.

"So, how was the sex education lesson?"

"Just okay."

"What did they teach you?"

"Male sex organs, female sex organs, safe sex, risk of unprotected sex, and risk of pregnancy."

"Anything else?"

"We also watched a video of a woman giving birth. That wasn't nice to watch."

"Why not?"

"There was so much blood. Why is there so much blood when a baby is delivered?"

"Because it's a traumatic experience for the body. It is not for the faint hearted. So, don't let anyone tell you that women are the weaker sex."

"Yeah, I believe that."

"Did they say anything about relationships?"

"No, but I already knew that from what you and Mum taught me."

A combination of naivety and wishful thinking had me conclude that we had all the bases covered. Almost two weeks went by before I realised that sex had become the main topic of discussion between him and his friends. They didn't need much motivation to research and share links to online material on the subject, some of which was inappropriate.

There was a perception among his age group that sex and love meant one and the same thing. It wasn't generally accepted that love was more about giving than receiving. Very few his age and even those much older were ready for the real thing, and neither was I in my teenage years, though I was none the wiser for it. There was a lot more on the line than just sexually transmitted diseases (STDs) and unwanted pregnancies. Casual sex could result in permanent ties that were not easy to discard.

My wife and I agreed there was a limit to how far the school could educate him about sex. They had only covered the mechanics and the most obvious risks. So, the onus was upon us to fill in the gaps. We dovetailed the basics of what he had learned with some lessons on values, relationships, and mutual respect. And we created opportunities to drive the same message home.

## Lifelong learning

At first he thought education only happened at school, college or university until he observed that his mother and I always appeared to be learning. The most important qualification he could gain from formal education was the urge to keep learning.

Technology, along with everything else around us, was changing at such a fast pace that skills could be outdated as soon as they were acquired. The software tools I used to develop solutions were upgraded every few months. And the diabetes knowledge base that his mother used in health education programmes could also be updated at any time. Staying up-to-date was, therefore, a full-time endeavour.

He was about 16, when one morning his mother told him that I had struggled to sleep the previous night, because I had not been well. Any expectations of sympathy were quickly extinguished.

"Don't worry about Dad, Mum. If he can't sleep, he will sit on his computer, rub his hands together in delight and do something on the SQL Server. He is fine."

# FOUR: MENTAL GRAFFITI

I was terrified by the ease with which a trespasser's imagery could be painted over a work of art. In the same vein, it didn't need much time or effort to hack into an impressionable mind.

The chances of nipping a problem in the bud were low as the odds were heavily stacked against us. We only had about two hours of meaningful engagement on school days. Everything hinged on communication, which turned out to be us mainly listening to what he wasn't saying.

### Low expectation

He was unusually quiet when I picked him from school one spring day during Year 2. At first, I assumed it was fatigue, but then I noticed that he was looking troubled.

When I asked him how the day had gone, he was ready to spill the beans. A teacher had singled him out for impromptu career guidance that morning.

"Your people are good with their hands," he was told. "When you grow up, look for a job that involves using your hands."

This didn't sit well with him, but he couldn't find the words to explain why. We agreed there was nothing wrong with the jobs the teacher was referring to. Somebody had to do them, out of choice. But there was everything wrong in the insinuation that only specific jobs were suitable for one race.

He understood the teacher was supposed to partner with his parents to bring out the best in him. But his advice had left him dejected. And he didn't think the teacher had treated him like the unique individual he knew he was.

I told him he had limitless potential, and no one could place a ceiling on who he could be. The school took the position that my son had probably misunderstood the teacher. It wasn't their policy to give career guidance to primary school pupils anyway. They assured me that the teacher would pay more attention to how he communicated.

It brought back unpleasant memories of his first year at nursery school in West London where a nursery school teacher had asked one of the aids to inform us that our son had learning difficulties.

I had spent enough time with him to know that his mind was razor sharp. So, I was more concerned about the impact it would have had on him had he found out.

The nursery school backtracked when we told them we intended to contact the council for more information. Unsurprisingly, by the time he left to go to the *big school*, he had become the standard against which others were measured and was the teacher's favourite.

So, I remained wary of the danger posed by low expectation. It was a silent killer that could turn a learning institution into a slaughter house of potential.

## Neighbourhood

When our son was in year 3, we lived in a decent West London neighbourhood. Young families were the main occupants of our apartment block. The place was safe enough to let him play in the back garden with friends.

I didn't consider the neighbourhood a threat until one morning on our way to school, he announced out of the blue, "When I grow up, I want to be a brother."

I had no idea what he meant.

He carried on. "I will have my own car. Hang out with my friends. I will have no homework. No job. Just have fun."

The penny dropped. He was describing the life of a young black man who lived with his mother in the flat above us. He had a car, didn't work, hung around with three young men of his age, and I called him *brother* because I just couldn't remember his name.

The *brother*, whose life he admired, happened to be the oldest black child in the immediate neighbourhood. Of course, he had a cushy lifestyle in the eyes of a seven-year-old.

We spoke at length about what success looked like and who he should look up to. But I had a hunch words alone were not adequate and thought a long overdue first visit to Zimbabwe could help him get acquainted with reality.

## Early perceptions of Africa

The planned visit to Zimbabwe excited him. It was going to be his first trip to Africa. He spoke about nothing else for weeks.

Even teachers and friends felt his excited anticipation as the end of school year approached. They had no idea what was in store for him. The little they knew about the continent was what usually made the headlines.

I was aware of how Africa's portrayal in mainstream media and pop culture could influence his self-perception. It wasn't uncommon even for the seemingly informed to refer to the continent as a country inhabited by a people of one culture, one mindset, and little potential.

I didn't notice anything unusual when I picked him up from school a few weeks before our trip. He was chatty all the way home. But as soon as we were inside, he started weeping. In between sobs, he announced he no longer wanted to go.

Though the U-turn took me by surprise, I calmly asked why. He was succinct and to the point: "Crocodiles".

I struggled to stifle a laugh and would have lost the battle had he looked up. It took me a few seconds to regain composure. Evidently, my wife and I had missed some clear signals.

A few months before, my wife's brother had unexpectedly died in Zimbabwe. She was distraught. It was our son's first experience of death in the family.

He innocently asked, "Was it the lions, Mum?"

She briefly put grief on pause to laugh before explaining that her brother had been ill.

He learned that neither his mother nor I had ever come across a crocodile in the wild and that we had only seen wild animals on guided tours. There only one way to correct the mental picture he had of how his people lived.

Two weeks later we touched down at the Harare International

Airport, giving our son, who had a window seat, his first glimpse of Zimbabwe and Africa.

He zeroed in on an airport luggage truck coming towards our plane. It was the driver and his two assistants that caught his attention.

"Oh my God, black men working!" he exclaimed.

We had not seen that coming. His mother enquired; "Haven't you seen black men at work in London?"

"Just at the Food Hall. Nowhere else." The Food Hall was an Afro-Caribbean market we frequented for fruits and vegetables.

It turned out his school had no black male teachers at the time. And when he spent the day at the office with me, he had seen that I was the only black man on a floor of over 60.

### Realistic goals

The sight of homeless children of all ages in the streets of Harare shook him. Every child had an untold story with a common end. He gave some of them food and money but sensed a lot more needed to be done.

Later he said, "When I grow up, I want to be the president of Zimbabwe. I want to help children."

We assured him he could be whoever he wanted to be and had absolutely no limitations.

Six years later, at high school, his class was asked to think about their careers. They each had to present their goals to the class. He thought he didn't need to prepare all that much as he knew exactly what he wanted to do.

His teacher was taken aback when he announced he wanted to be the president of Zimbabwe but gave no context.

"You need to be realistic about your goal," the teacher warned. "You must aim for something you can actually be."

He sounded disheartened when he related the incident to me that evening.

He had learned two important lessons: the need to prepare presentations with an audience in mind and to be selective about whom he shared his innermost dreams with.

He was relieved to find out he didn't have to wait to be president to look out for the less fortunate. He could follow the lead set by London-based Zimbabwean entrepreneur and philanthropist, Strive Masiyiwa, whose scholarships has helped over 100,000 young Africans. In addition, he has provided for the needs of over 40,000 orphans and generously contributed to the fight against the Ebola virus in parts of Africa.

## Teased for his dark skin

Playground dynamics at the mixed-race West London school were totally different from those in the predominantly white middle-class South London school he had moved to just before he became a teenager.

One evening he had a heart-to-heart with his mother before I got home from work.

"Mum, it's not that I mind being black. I am proud of my race. But I wish I were as light as you."

It's no wonder he didn't come to me first, being the culprit of his colour situation.

His mother quickly confessed, "I love dark skin. I actually wish I were darker. There is absolutely nothing wrong with your complexion."

When my wife replayed the dialogue to me, I wondered what had brought it about and who had said what to him.

It turned out that he had been teased about his dark skin at school and called *darky*. Lighter black boys had been spared.

"It wasn't racist, Dad," he attempted to calm me down.

"Did they also tease any white boy?"

"Yeah. We called him *creamy*."

He thought he knew what racism looked like and concluded what had happened wasn't racist, because a white boy had also been on the receiving end. The impact it had on him was evidence that it wasn't a laughing matter and couldn't be taken lightly, whatever the cause.

Moreover, it wasn't an isolated incident, he realised upon reflection. One afternoon, when the classroom lights were turned off to watch an educational video, it gave someone the green light to shout from across the room, "Hey, where is Ruvhi?" And to another, it gave the liberty to add, "Smile, Ruvhi!" What the whole class took for harmless banter ate him from the inside under the cover of darkness.

For me, it was déjà vu. I had also been teased about the colour of my skin and had a nickname, *Demadema* (very dark), that went with it. A family member had given it to me during my formative years in pre-independence Zimbabwe. Much as I hated the nickname, I never resented the colour of my skin.

We agreed that he was neither going to participate in name calling, nor was he going to tolerate it. So, he took it upon himself to have a few one-to-ones with the main instigators. I was not privy to how he approached it. But whatever he did put a lid on the matter without our intervention.

## Friends with no ambition

Parents' evening was like a scripted annual performance. The drama began to unfold the evening before when we confirmed appointment times with his teachers. Typically, there would be a worried look on his face that would be quickly replaced by a brave front when queried.

None of the feedback we got from his teachers took us by surprise. It was a summary of term-wide communication.

But his Year 9 history teacher's feedback had a new dimension.

"Your son is very ambitious. But he hangs around with boys who have no ambition at all. He must cut them loose."

It was a white teacher, referring to two of his friends.

Being at the same station at the same time didn't mean everyone was headed the same way, I pointed out. As a first-generation *settler* in London, we knew that he needed to work harder than his peers.

Real wealth is passed from one generation to the next. There are no short cuts. History had confined him to playing catch-up. He knew that he had no rich relative to inherit from. So, he couldn't afford to let opportunities pass him by.

# FIVE: RACISM UNDER THE MICROSCOPE

### Racist slur

The eve of the last day of our son's first year at high school was unforgettable. That day, I didn't notice anything unusual about him when I got home from work. Then a family friend phoned.

I was told that our son had been on the receiving end of a racist slur that afternoon. He was so incensed that he was going to fight the culprit the following day after school. I was thankful for the information.

When I confronted him with the facts, he filled in the gaps. A girl was at the centre of the altercation. *How daft*, I concluded in my mind, even before all the facts were in.

The other boy didn't take rejection lightly. Pointing a finger at my son, he mocked the girl, "How could you pick this *freshie* over me?"

Red mist descended. There was posturing. Threats were

exchanged. I was out of touch with the lingo and needed interpretation.

"It means fresh off a boat, like a slave ship," he explained, gesturing with open palms, probably expecting to receive understanding of his rage and even endorsement for the fight.

But he had allowed himself to get dragged to the brink of the wrong fight, creating a lose–lose situation for himself. Even if he beat his adversary, he would still lose: I knew that physically hurting anyone was going to mentally torture him. And there was the risk of having a permanent police record that he wouldn't be able to erase or wish away.

After half an evening of reality check, we finally agreed that not even the wronged have the right of way at the anger intersection. Caution was always required. Even in the heat of the moment, he had a choice. The best option was for him to report the matter to the school authorities, which he did first thing the following day.

The anticipated fight would not have happened, anyway. The other boy didn't turn up for school.

### ABC of racism

My son's encounter with racism was inevitable. There was no way to shield him. An incident of racism, real or perceived, even in a distant part of the world, could have the same effect as a direct encounter. He could get just as riled up by the racist abuse of a black player in a football stadium on the other side of the world.

So, we reasoned that a thorough understanding of the scourge could prepare him to respond appropriately instead of reacting blindly. He learned that the racism pendulum swung between two extremes, one of which attributed every disparity to racism, whilst the other committed itself to cast doubt over its existence. Reality was not always an in-between.

The roots of racism are rarely exposed. They mostly lie dormant under the surface and are even known to shrink during times of plenty. But uncertainty and economic downturns precipitate re-growth and bring fresh offshoots.

Courts of law are only empowered to deal with offshoots. There is no legislation to uproot this vice. So, more energy is devoted towards avoiding being perceived as racist than dealing with the underlying racism. Pruning offshoots and leaving the roots intact has the predictable effect of stimulating growth.

Racism sets the perpetrator's race as a bar of excellence. It preaches the superiority of the white race and promotes self-loathing in young and impressionable black men and women. It often lurks beneath a thin veneer of friendship and politeness from where it magnifies every negative trait in the supposed inferior and either dismisses or claims credit for every positive one. And so effective has been the promotion of the white saviour narrative that many more than is generally assumed subconsciously acquiesce to white supremacy.

For many a black boy, without fully understanding why, the battle for life is a skirmish to stay off the bottom of the barrel.

### Root of racism

The root of racism is a sincere belief in the superiority of one's own race. Though it is generally thought that only the unpol-ished fan the flames of racism, facts on the ground show that certain academics from different eras set the stage.

The 18th century Scottish philosopher David Hume was quoted as saying, "I am apt to suspect the Negroes to be naturally inferior to the Whites. There scarcely ever was a civilised nation of that complexion, nor even any individual, eminent either in action or in speculation. No ingenious manufacture among them, no arts, no sciences."

The German philosopher, George Friedrich Hegel, in the 19th century, also remarked: "Africa is no historical part of the world; it has no movement or development to exhibit." This was echoed by the Oxford History professor, Hugh Trevor-Roper who, in 1963, said, "There is only the history of Europeans in Africa. The rest is darkness."

Academic freedom has recently been used as a launching pad of theories grounded in racial inequality. In 2006, Satoshi Kanazawa, an evolutionary psychologist at the London School of Economics, published a paper that alleged African states were poor and suffered chronic ill-health because their populations were less intelligent than people in richer countries.

And James Watson, a renowned US scientist and Nobel Prize winner, claimed in 2007 that black people were less intelligent than white people and that the idea that "equal powers of reason" were shared across racial groups was a delusion.

After convincing myself that no one in their right mind would take any such views seriously, I was shocked when a pastor of a multicultural church in South London, someone I had known for a long time, asked me in 2015, "If Africans are as smart as you claim, why are they poor?"

I later told him I would invite him and his wife to Zimbabwe when convenient. He had never been to Africa. Despite the risk that he would see only what he wanted to see, I had no doubt a first-hand experience would still be educational.

## Bounty

One evening, during his second year in high school, my son was visibly annoyed when I got home from work. His friends, both black and white, had called him a bounty.

Admitting my failure to keep up with the evolving language, I once again had to ask what it meant.

"It's a chocolate that's dark on the outside and white inside."

They told him he didn't dress *black*, didn't behave *black*, and neither did he speak *black*. And that made him white inside.

Up to that point I was guilty of influencing both his dressing sense and spoken language. I had discouraged common colloquialisms from entering his vocabulary early in life – not to whiten him, but to help him learn the language well enough to be able to intentionally break its rules. How he conducted himself was entirely his choice.

The stereotypical picture of a black boy in his friends' minds betrayed a belief that some natural behaviour was inherently white and could only be imitated by other races.

He was surprised that his friends were surprised he found it offensive. The experience was educational in different ways to both parties. His friends could choose to never walk the path again, but my son could only respond.

## Silent offence

Silence or saying (and doing) nothing when something ought to be said or done can be just as offensive as the vilest abuse.

Just before an evening meal with the fellow trusties of a charity organisation in South London, a colleague I had only known for a few months announced, "I had a fantastic day. I was with Jeff – the only lateral-thinking African I know."

The words hit me like a hammer to the head. To my surprise, the shock wasn't mutual. I could as well have been the only one who had heard what was said.

I challenged him, "What exactly do you mean?"

He had lived and worked in South Africa all his life and had only moved to England after retirement. So, it wasn't as if he had only known a handful of Africans.

He wouldn't look me in the eye, nor did he explain himself even after I repeated the question. Everyone else in the room saw a funny side to it that I had totally missed. After a good laugh, the chairman shifted attention to the business of the day without any further reference to the matter.

This incident put paid to the notion that having a black friend was a cure of the racism bug. Silence spoke more eloquently than the words uttered and implied. I made a mental note to remember to guide my son about whom he shouldn't look up to.

### Public racist abuse

He found out from an early age that his first favourite sport, football, was never too far from the controversy of racism. Fans abusing black players was commonplace in Europe. But in the minds of many, the abuse was no more offensive than the mockery fans were licensed to dish out.

Perhaps it wasn't common knowledge that the perpetrators might as well have been hurling abuse at every black boy that loved the game enough to watch it. My son internalised it from the time he was old enough to understand what it meant. Every "monkey" chant was an attempt to downgrade historical human rights abuse against Africa's people to the lesser crime of cruelty against animals.

No country's football association thought they were at the bottom of the racism league, but none knew how the plague could be effectively dealt with.

Football authorities wanted to believe racism couldn't possibly breach the barriers of stadium terraces to corrupt the very heart of football. But the line between objectivity and subjectivity could easily be crossed and the burden of proof of wrongdoing placed on the victims' shoulders.

By his early teens, he had fallen out with the game altogether for a number of reasons. Instead he felt drawn to the glamour of basketball.

### Nigger

My son was one of the several black boys in the school basketball team. Whenever one of them played well, a black boy he wasn't particularly close to would shout, "That's my nigger!"

He was surprised by the ease with which the word slipped out of his teammate's mouth. It caused him much discomfort. His friends knew him well enough to notice it annoyed him.

Unfortunately, the other boy was oblivious to my son's reaction. So, he persisted and used variations of the *compliment*, always with the word nigger thrown in.

He was neither friendly enough with the boy nor bold enough to explain why he thought it was inappropriate. So, he suffered in silence. I didn't intervene or offer suggestions.

Three years later, when he joined a predominantly black college basketball team, I asked him if anyone ever used the term.

"Oh yeah, all the time," he answered.

"Don't you still find it offensive?"

"No. When it's just us, it's calm. There is no risk of misunderstanding what it means."

"And in high school?"

"I was afraid white boys would think it was okay to cross the line and say it after hearing it from a teammate."

"Why didn't you say something to your high school teammate?"

"I assumed he knew. And even if I wanted to, I didn't know where to start."

He had long known that nigger is more than just a word. It is synonymous with a permanent underclass, an embodiment of inferiority, and used as a justification of historical injustice. But in the very private world of black boys, it means defiance. It is a call to take it on the chin and excel, in spite of.

## Endgame

It was important that my son clearly understood the endgame of the fight against racism. Some quarters perceived (and still do) that reverse racism is justifiable and fighting fire with fire is the way to go. Then there is the idealistic picture of acceptance by others as an equal.

We instilled in him that his endgame was self-acceptance. It wasn't his place to try to change minds set in their ways. Pulling down people made racists experience illusions of elevation, lulling them into believing that they didn't need to change.

The only mind he could work on was his. He was taught over time to love who he was, to cherish his heritage, to feel

completely comfortable in his own skin, and to count his bless-
ings, at the top of which was his uniqueness, and to make each
one of them count.

It was drummed into him that he could never give what he didn't
have, so he could only appreciate other people to the degree that
he valued himself.

To bring out the best in him, he was urged to look for something
he loved in every person, and he found out that the best in
everyone was just below the surface and didn't need much
excavation.

At 17, he stated, "I don't know if I feel more pity than annoyance
towards racists."

When he stumbled upon black pride, one of the many defences
against racism, I felt compelled to help him dissect it. He found
out that no single slogan could ever express its essence and that
nothing could eloquently communicate black pride better than
the quality of services provided to our own by our own.

# SIX: PROTECTION

I spent more time pondering over how best to protect him than anything else. The battle would have been much easier had we always fought on the same side, but the higher the stakes, the less we could collaborate.

Though we agreed his safety was paramount, we never could see eye to eye on the way forward. Things got complicated in his mid-teens when he started feeling safe in dangerous situations. To compound matters, he thought he knew how best to protect himself.

## Boundaries

Virtual boundaries were erected around him and enforced as best as we could. He knew the rationale behind and the implications of crossing each one of them. But it didn't dissuade him from tiptoeing across them from time to time. So, I picked my battles. I had neither the energy nor the time to fight them all. In the end, the goal was to catch him within the mutually agreed boundaries.

At the end of his first day in high school, he told me, "I think this is your kind of school, Dad. You will like it. There is discipline."

The principal had apparently set clear boundaries. Though he didn't admit it, it was apparent he felt secure in the set boundaries.

After his 'A' levels, he singled out his College Software Development teacher as his favourite. The teacher had full control of his classes, and everyone knew better than to go on his wrong side.

### Words

Negative words, spoken and unspoken, were my son's top threat. They are the highest killer of potential in black boys and could eat him inside without anyone noticing.

Weaponised words, however softly packaged, could be deadly. And the older he grew, the better he understood what wasn't said. For instance, no words needed to be uttered for him to understand that the past was often portrayed as a roadmap to the future of the average black boy.

Retractions, no matter how well-intentioned or sincere, could not completely undo serious damage. So, the fight could not just be reactive. Only the right kind of education would do. As academic freedom was used to lay a few landmines in the form of flawed racial inequality theories in his path, he was taught to assume responsibility for what he was learning.

### Carbohydrates

His next highest threat was carbohydrates. He was not genetically equipped to stomach a carbs-heavy diet. Unlike him, his white peers had a higher tolerance. One only had to look at the higher prevalence of Type 2 Diabetes amongst the Afro-Caribbean in comparison to their Caucasian counterparts.

Although he knew he couldn't eat the same quantities as everyone else, his taste buds occasionally overruled his caution. When he was seven, he enquired, "Why are foods that are no good for you so yummy?"

The dangers posed by cheap sugary snacks were highlighted to him whenever warning signs surfaced. The battle against carbs typified his frontline defence for self-control. Once breached, other battles would be tougher.

An unexplainable weight-increase in his second-year in high school triggered alarm bells in my head. He was sporty, ate well at home, and took a 30-minute uphill walk to school daily. There was no reason for him to put on weight. It could only be unhealthy snacks, I reasoned.

The mystery was solved when his mother and I took a day off work one Friday. Unbeknown to us, a friend's mother picked him up every morning to drive him and his friend to school. His weight normalised within three weeks of resuming the uphill walk. But that was only part of the problem. He had developed a sweet tooth and kept a stash of snacks hidden in his room.

Thanks to his mother, a Nutrition Advisor and Diabetes Nurse Consultant, there was nothing he didn't know about the danger posed by obesity and diabetes. But knowing was one thing and acting on it a different matter altogether. He needed help to stay on track.

We ensured his home meals were balanced, regularly checked his room for contraband, repeatedly drummed home the same message about healthy eating habits, and even went for early morning runs with him. We could not, however, declare a lasting victory against the formidable foe.

It was easier to go off track than to stay on it. A few days' holiday on the other side had the potential to derail months of discipline. In his first year at university, the weight slowly crept back on unnoticed, until one day he realised he was overweight. It took months of concerted effort on his part to get back on track. A combination of intermittent fasting, increased activity, and reduction of readymade meals and snacks gradually normalised his weight.

## Blind following

Blind following was a worrying threat on two fronts. Too many who were eager to lead him had nowhere to take him. And he had shown a willingness to follow anyone who stood out from others, even if it was for the wrong reasons, during his initial years in high school.

"You can't just follow anyone, son. You should only follow someone that can be led – a teachable person."

Someone who had no awareness of their own need to learn could not lead anyone anywhere worthwhile.

That he was heading in the wrong direction was often signalled by a sudden loss of interest in an important extracurricular activity or the taking up of a new hobby unrelated to his aspirations just to fit in with the in-crowd.

It wasn't as if he didn't understand the futility of blind following. He just thought he had plenty of time to take a U-turn when convenient. But he soon learned that most wrong roads don't have a detour, and once he was on one of them, the only way out would be a rescue. I, therefore, stayed ready.

He learned that blind loyalty to political leaders and political parties accounted for much of Africa's woes. So, caution was required of every demand for blind loyalty in school play-grounds, in the neighbourhood, in workplaces, and even in the Church.

It was worth noting that it wasn't just sexual abuse that tarnished the image of the Church. The futile attempt to close ranks to cover it up was more damaging.

In his late teens, he picked up that nothing was exempt from scrutiny. We encouraged him to question the validity of every-thing, even the very things we taught him.

### Substance abuse

The battle against substance abuse started before he turned ten. We had countless chats about drugs, alcohol, and smoking. He grew up in an alcohol, drugs, and smoke-free home. Though it has been proven that alcohol in moderation isn't a bad thing, it wasn't for us.

Lectures by themselves couldn't do the trick. I could tell when he mentally switched off. Around the age of ten, I took him to the backstreets of a nearby shopping complex, where he saw for himself the end-result of alcohol and substance abuse.

Movies were a great way to reinforce the message. Family favourites like *To Sir, with Love II*, *Lean on Me*, and *Coach Carter* drove the message home. I was confident he wouldn't experi-ment with drugs.

After his "A" levels, he told me in passing that one of his former class mates, *a very nice guy*, sold drugs in college. I didn't expect him to mention "nice guy" and "drug dealer" in the same sentence.

"His mum worked all the time for very little, and he wanted to help."

"Where did his mother think he got the money?"

"Part-time job, I suppose."

"How come you never said anything before?"

"I didn't want to create problems for myself."

"What problems?"

"You would have been onto me for just knowing someone that dealt drugs."

"How is he a nice guy?"

"He gets on well with everyone. The only time I saw him lose it was when one boy borrowed money from him and didn't pay him back the day he promised."

"What did he do?"

"He went mad. He is a tiny guy. But he went so mad even his facial features changed. He surprised me."

"Was he on drugs?"

"I don't think so. I thought he was in it just for the money."

"And what were the other boys in it for?"

### Violence

Violence among black boys was a topical issue in our household. Being aware that dialogue alone could not keep him safe kept me on high alert. It compelled me to dissect almost every violence-based tragedy with him – something he tolerated in the beginning but gradually grew to resent.

It wasn't immediately apparent to him or his peers that the loss of a young life indiscriminately robbed the whole community of potential. Even the families of the perpetrators suffered unimaginable loss. Grief is communal, and it can take the average parent days, weeks, months or even years to take in an avoidable loss of life. I had not anticipated that raising him would run parallel to dealing with so much grief.

I remained protective towards him even when he grew to be 6ft 5" and became physically stronger than me. Inside this seemingly formidable mass of flesh and muscle was still my boy – a largely compassionate young man. The only time he allowed himself to get dragged to the brink of a fight saw us devoting half an evening to some serious soul-searching.

Soaring incidences of knife crime in the capital kept me on edge. What disturbed me most was what it took to override the conscience of many a black boy. I was certain none had been born that way and confident that their supreme instinct was to live and even thrive.

"Why don't you think increasing police presence on the streets would help?" he wondered, after I'd expressed my reservations about it.

To me, the need for higher police presence was only a symptom of the real problem – hopelessness. A police force was only equipped to deal with the symptoms. And the numbers required to prevent every violent crime were just not feasible.

Unfortunately, that wasn't the only issue at hand. The boys were in a state of war, at least in their minds. So, they took their cues from real military conflict.

It didn't help that the preparedness to kill millions, either in *self-defence* or as a pre-emptive measure, was considered a sign of strong leadership, and hesitancy of any sort, an unforgivable weakness.

Whilst he had been taught about the sacredness of human life (all life) from an early age, this notion wasn't universally embraced. Different yardsticks could be used to grade human life. Loss of one life could be deemed a tragedy, whilst the loss of another was viewed as cause for celebration. So, he got used to swimming against the tide.

We used every available opportunity to give him reasons to hope for a better tomorrow and left it to him to build on the foundation.

# SEVEN: FREEDOM

Most of the conflict between my son and me revolved around his quest for more freedom. He was convinced everyone he knew had a lot more and life was passing him by, thanks to my acute awareness of hazards.

The primary source of conflict was our differing views on his level of maturity. He thought he was wiser than his years, but I was certain he didn't know what he didn't know. So, he almost always felt short-changed.

As a *big yute*, he was used to being mistaken as older. He was amused when, at 15, a friendly shop assistant asked him which university he attended. He soon took everyone's cue and began conducting himself like he was older.

At the ripe age of 16, he sat his mother and me down one weekend and maturely stated, "You know what, I just want to thank you for not allowing me to go out when I was young. Some of the boys and girls that did are messed up now..."

His mother smiled with pride, thinking our boy had at last seen the light. But my antenna went up. I had distinctly heard him announce he had joined the ranks of the grown-ups. Although he didn't know it yet, wisdom had a much slower pace than physical growth. The challenge was to convince him that he still had some growing up to do.

### Man-to-man chat

To clear the air, I thought it would help to at least agree on what we disagreed about.

"What do you think freedom is?" I asked him at breakfast one Saturday morning.

"Basically, it's being able to do what I want when I choose."

"Such as?"

"Going out, hanging out with my friends, you know, things like that."

"Don't you already do that?"

"Yeah, but because I have to get back early, I am the first to leave all the time. Everyone knows I have the strictest dad."

It wasn't our first time on that path. Weeks before he had expressed similar frustrations: "Dad, you and I both know you are overprotective."

I didn't dispute that, neither did we disagree on the reality of the spectre of violence that hung over black boys in London. But regurgitating the facts could overshadow what I had in mind that morning.

Dragging the discussion back to the theme, I asked him, "Would you say one of the keys to freedom is being able to make choices like who to hang out with, what time to get back home, the quality of life you will lead when you eventually leave home, et cetera?"

"Yeah, I'd say that."

Feigning a closure to the discussion, I said, "It's good to know."

He wasn't ready to let it go and probed, "What do you think?"

"For me, freedom has two facets. On one side are exercisable choices, and on the other, wisdom."

"Aren't all choices exercisable?"

"Not to the same degree for everyone. A social drinker can choose when to have a beer and when not to. Right?"

"Yeah."

"Would you say an alcoholic has the same latitude?"

"No."

"As far as I know, you don't take drugs, right?"

Shaking his head, he said, "You know I don't."

"Can a drug addict abstain from the habit for a week?"

"Okay, I see the logic. So, is what you're calling wisdom knowing what the best option is in every situation?"

"It's more than just knowing. It is the application of what you know that makes wisdom."

"At what age do you think I'll be wise enough to make my own decisions?"

"It has little to do with age. You'll be wise enough when you are able to weigh the implications of every option, know your limitations and who to trust."

We agreed the best options were gateways to more exercisable choices, and the worst, to little or no choice. Any form of addiction, i.e., alcohol, drugs, nicotine, sex, food, and video games, amongst others, would limit his choices and compromise his freedom.

Even then, he wasn't entirely convinced that what he took for restrictions were in fact safeguards.

## Forgiveness

Blind reaction to offence or injustice could potentially hold him captive to the conduct of others. Left unchecked, his daily agenda could be set for him. A measured response to every contentious situation was the only way he could remain on his chosen path.

He didn't consider forgiveness an effective response and thought it could be easily mistaken for a soft centre. So, he only reserved it for family and his inner circle. The image of forgiveness he held in his mind was sketchy in comparison to the glossy picture of revenge that promised instant gratification.

I was worried revenge could ensnare him in a vicious cycle of score settling. And once in, there was no easy way out. It fuelled the cycle of violence in the city. An atrocity on one side was met with another on the other side.

Once upon a time, I had a different set of worries. I vividly remember the day a bigger boy picked on him in the school playground during Year 1. The boy had all the attributes of a bully. I disliked and wrote him off at first sight. Vowing to keep tabs on the matter, I warned my son to keep his distance from the bully.

I couldn't believe it when a few days later, the two came out of class together, all smiles, arms around each other's shoulder, and ran straight to me. As if nothing had ever happened between the two, he introduced the boy to me, "Dad, this is my best friend, Hugh." Did I feel like a mug then?

Times had changed. Few wrongs were considered unforgivable in his world. Perceived disrespect, even without proof, was one of them.

In his later years, we discussed one of the greatest freedom fighters of all time, Nelson Mandela, the first president of independent South Africa. He learned that very few people in the world had suffered more injustice than Mandela, who was sentenced to life in prison for aspiring to create a just society for his nation.

When released 27 years later, he understood he didn't have to be in custody to be in prison and famously said, "As I walked out the door toward the gate that would lead to my freedom, I knew if I didn't leave my bitterness and hatred behind, I'd still be in prison."

Forgiveness cancelled yesterday's march from today's parade and freed the wronged to set a fresh programme. It was essential to keep yesterday on a leash: If it went out of control, it could hold today hostage.

The decision to forgive was not dependent on contriteness, neither was it dictated by emotions. So, it was made before there was a need for it.

The greatest teacher of all time, Jesus Christ, proclaimed he came to set the captives free. It was no coincidence that forgiveness was central to his teachings. He brought out the best in the most unlikely people by wiping the slate clean.

I could deduce from my son's demeanour and tone that he was at the very least going to consider it. Fishing for a reaction from me, he asked, "Dad, isn't forgiveness really about letting someone off the hook?"

"Yes. It is about letting yourself off the hook, Son."

## Fear

Fear, if not managed, could leave him without choice. It was a subtle threat to his freedom. He found out early on that fear shepherded people from behind. It created a sense of urgency and demanded immediate action with limited information.

Most of his fears were easy to allay when he was younger. He looked up to me for answers, so his fears were brought out into the open. But the fears got more complex as he grew older. Most pertained to his safety and demanded decisions on the go.

At the age of 14, he had a week's work placement at a children's centre in a deprived neighbourhood, to which he travelled by train before taking a 10-minute walk from the station.

One morning, on his walk to the centre, he noticed two older boys, one on a bike and the other on foot, coming from the opposite direction on a quiet road. Fear gripped him and, as a precaution, he quickly took off his headphones. Unfortunately, it hadn't gone unnoticed. When he was close enough, one of the two boys confronted him.

"Why did you take off your headphones?"

"To call my dad," he explained, indicating the phone in his hand.

The pair looked at each other and seemed to nonverbally agree the explanation was reasonable.

"That's cool," said the interrogator before the two went on their way.

I was reacquainted with fear when he called immediately after the encounter. Most children his age had heard stories of muggings, and he therefore knew the risks of being in the wrong place at the wrong time.

Had it not been that he only had one more day to complete the placement, I would have reconsidered his travel arrangements. He politely declined the centre's offer to drive him to and from the station.

Three years later, he had grown bigger and attended a different college than some of his high school friends. One Saturday, he and four (white) high school friends decided to hang out at a nearby shopping complex.

One of them noticed a large group of black boys, walking side-by-side and covering the whole street, coming towards them. There was no way to avoid them. It was too late to do a U-turn without attracting unwanted attention.

"What shall we do?" one of his friends asked him.

"This doesn't look good. I am not looking to get robbed," said the other.

My son took a close look at the approaching group and assured his friends, "Don't worry about it. It should be okay." Though he didn't explain why, they had no option but to man up and head towards what could be trouble.

As they drew closer to the other group, conversation stopped, and direct eye-contact was avoided. They couldn't wait for the moment to pass to start breathing. So, they were shocked to hear my son provoke the group, "What are you looking at?!"

Much to their relief, he knew most of the boys from his new college. They exchanged greetings like long-lost relatives before going their separate ways. He told me he understood why anyone

that didn't know them could be afraid. But behind the intimi-
dating appearance and boisterous attitudes were ordinary boys
with whom he shared common fears that included personal
safety, failure, limited opportunities, uncertain future, being
misunderstood, and injustice.

For every fear identified, I helped him prepare for the worst
whilst building hope for the best outcome. It kept all exercisable
options on the table and allowed him to retain control.

### Love

"Can I help who I fall in love with?" he asked one evening, just
before he turned 18.

"Do you have a girlfriend now?" The investigator in me sprang to
life.

He generally found it annoying whenever I responded to a question with a question. If he was, he didn't let it show.

"Not serious enough to bring her to meet you."

Contrary to the central theme in popular stories, love is a daily
choice, I told him. It is often confused with infatuation, which is
transient.

The happily-ever-after ending in movies is only the start of the
real thing, which is a lifetime of hard work. It was only fair he
had the freedom to pick and choose who he was going to love.

He observed that his mother and I were different. She had an
abundance of patience with him, whilst my reserves were often
low. I was very risk averse about where he went at night, but she
seemed very relaxed about it. He observed that his mother took
the things he said on face value, whilst I tended to probe deep to
unearth what he wasn't saying.

He picked up that our marriage was based on common values, not our similarities, and that we had more strengths because of our differences. I told him that the person I had been when I had first met his mother would not have attracted her 25 years later, and neither would I be impressed with the girl I had met those many moons ago. Neither of us had stood still. We had changed, adapted, and grown together. And I was more content with the woman she evolved into each day.

Potential had more promise than what seemed to be the finished product. It was best he made his choice based on the woman she was likely to become rather than the girl she was today. Only then would he find love liberating enough to bring out the best in him.

## Symbols of freedom

When he failed to find a t-shirt with an appropriate symbol of freedom, he decided to design one, but couldn't make up his mind what the best symbol was. None of the images he stumbled upon spoke to him, neither was he impressed with the notion that owning a gun could be considered a symbol of freedom.

He understood why national flags and monuments like the Statue of Liberty could be regarded as symbols of freedom. But the freedom he had in mind was not just political.

I suggested taking a closer look at a story in the Bible that was almost as old as time, a story he already knew. In the second chapter of Genesis, we read that God created the first man, Adam, whom He placed in the Garden of Eden, an orchard like no other. God gave Adam permission to eat fruit from all other trees except from the tree of knowledge of good and evil.

So, to Adam, the tree of knowledge of good and evil symbolised exercisable choices. It even presented a gateway to rebel against his creator. The dilemma it presented may have blinded him from recognising the priceless gift of free will that he had.

When Adam and Eve eventually ate from the tree, there was no way back, no U-turn. Innocence was lost forever. It was one of those options that, once taken, wiped away all other choices from the table.

Tragic as it was, it wasn't unanticipated. A way out had already been choreographed before Adam was even created. So, loss of innocence set in motion a series of events told in the Old Testament leading to the birth of God's son, Jesus Christ, in human form. His mission was to reconcile humanity with God.

His crucifixion, death, and subsequent resurrection are the cornerstones of Christian faith. Without resurrection, there would be no Christianity, which makes the Easter story more significant than Christmas.

He concluded that the tree of knowledge of good and evil was the first symbol of freedom. And the cross, which depicted Christ's death and resurrection, was even more significant. It symbolises the Creator's amnesty to humanity's natural tendency to self-destruct. It is open to anyone, but it isn't for everyone.

He noted that faith, just like fear, was also a shepherd. Instead of driving people from behind, it led from the front, presenting choice all the time.

# EIGHT: PRESUMPTION OF GUILT

Though he knew right from wrong and stayed on the straight and narrow, there was no guarantee justice would always be on his side. And there was no way to predict which of the many faces of justice he could encounter. So, we learned to mind the gap between the public portrait of justice and the different images he could come across in the streets. We could only hope he would never have to contend with the presumption of guilt.

### Tsotsi

I was keen to hear my South African work colleague's thoughts after my family and I watched the movie, *Tsotsi*, set in her country. Though she had heard of it, she was yet to watch it.

"Do you know what *tsetse* means?" I asked.

"It's a young black boy," she promptly replied.

I desperately tried not to look shocked. *Tsotsi* was one of the many words adopted from South Africa that had become a part of Zimbabwe's everyday language.

"It means a petty thief or criminal," I stated.

"I always thought it meant a young black boy. We grew up calling all black boys *tsotsis* at my grandparents' farm."

Whether or not she knew what it meant didn't really matter. Every black boy understood it perfectly. Hence, the majority instinctively carried the heavy burden of proving innocence – a burden black boys in urban centres worldwide perfectly understood. Indifference wasn't an option.

### Supermarket alarm

He was almost 12 when he had his first taste of the wrong end of presumption of guilt. Our local supermarket's anti-shoplifting alarm went off as we were leaving the place one busy Saturday morning.

Up to three groups of shoppers, including my family and I, stopped, but two or three carried on and left. The security guard asked my family and I to come back inside but allowed the other shoppers, all white, to go on their way.

I politely asked why we had been singled out but didn't get a satisfactory explanation. An elderly black lady who had seen what had happened suspended shopping to stand by us. When it turned out that it wasn't our trolley that had triggered the alarm, the elderly lady pointed her walking stick at the security guard, brought it down hard, and shouted, "And you let the *t'ief* go."

The manager on duty apologised but had no answer to the only question I had. On the way home, my son enquired, "Did that man think we are shoplifters because we are black?"

Only the security guard, also black, could give a definitive answer.

## High school lesson in justice

One evening, I arrived home from work and stepped into what felt like an ambush. My son, then thirteen, had been lying in wait to set my agenda for the evening.

Pacing up and down the lobby, he exclaimed, "Dad, you will never guess what happened at school today! I'm telling you – you will never guess."

I mentally dismissed the possibility that he had been in trouble, otherwise he wouldn't be that dramatic. Sitting down, I gave him the impression he had my full attention (though half my mind was still at work).

"The police were at school today."

It quickly brought back all my focus into the room. They had come to carry out inspections of all students. He had first thought that students were randomly separated into two lines when his two white friends were asked to join one line, and his black friend and he, the other. Then he noticed his line largely had ethnic minorities, both boys and girls, and the only whites in the line were known troublemakers. The school must have provided some intel, he reasoned.

Whilst all bags were electronically scanned, only students in his line were body searched. There was an immediate uproar from the ethnic minority students. None of them had signed up for the fast-track lesson in street justice. Some immediately accused the police of racism. Reliving the happenings of the day brought raw emotions to the surface.

"I don't mind that I was searched. But can you imagine they put me in the same group as known troublemakers."

The school had become a place of a different kind of education that day. And it was a big deal to him what every student had learned. White students could conclude that they were generally presumed innocent and that it was permissible to treat ethnic minorities differently. And ethnic minority students, particularly black boys, had their first taste of prejudice, and could expect more of the same in the future.

It was as good a time as any to bring him up to speed with justice realities of the day. National statistics showed youth jails in England and Wales had a 40% representation of black boys, quite disproportionate for a people that made up less than 5% of the population.

But that wasn't the only uncomfortable statistic. He was also 28 times more likely to be stopped and searched than his white counterparts. Knife crime in the city had gone up, and most perpetrators looked like him.

The numbers and what had happened at school that day sowed the first seeds of mistrust in the justice system in his mind. Despite everything, it was important he knew how to conduct himself in potential brushes with the police. And the better he understood the terrain, the easier it would be for him to drive in the safe lane.

I was happy he had politely cooperated and complied with what was asked of him that day. It wasn't in his interests to view the police as his enemies.

I urged him to expect every police officer to treat him fairly and accord him the same level of respect he gave them.

It wasn't a gamble. Though there were exceptions in rogue police officers, he was likely to find what he expected. And more important, it made it easier for him to detect disparities.

## One-man protest

This sense of injustice compelled him to stage a one-man protest. Despite my misgivings, he was taken in by the coolness of wearing a hoodie, the so-called official uniform of crime.

That he could be stopped and searched and suspected of a crime yet to be committed didn't appear to bother him at all. My wife asked me to exercise the patience I didn't have.

He next found the belt irrelevant and wore his trousers so low he had to keep his shirt out to cover his underpants. The look's US-prison origin and the impression he made took a back seat to his protest against the normalisation of racial profiling.

Though he had made himself a perfect stop-and-search candidate, the first-hand experience in the streets eluded him throughout his teens.

## Taste of injustice

A black man was shot dead on either side of his 14th birthday during a defining six-month period for him. He closely followed both cases, which dominated international news channels for different reasons.

A few months before he turned 14, police shot and killed Mark Duggan in North London during an arrest. The tragedy was followed by conflicting accounts of what had happened.

Duggan's family and friends refuted initial media reports that he was armed and staged a peaceful demonstration at a North London police station. Suspicion of a police cover-up drew scores of sympathisers to the demonstration, which transformed into an expression of anger.

Community leaders' appeal for calm to allow the investigation to proceed was not heeded. The idea of the police investigating themselves did not inspire much confidence. This mood quickly descended into rioting, looting, and destruction of property. Each day saw temperatures rise to new levels as different parts of the city adopted the cause. Chaos spread even further when other cities took the cue and followed suite. Five lives were lost, and property worth millions of pounds was destroyed.

The narrative then changed from tragic loss of life to calls for restoration of order and more robust policing. Justice obliged and moved swiftly to arrest more than 2,000 and charge over 1,000 with riot-related crimes in less than two weeks.

My son and I couldn't understand why the wheels of justice didn't turn just as fast to bring Duggan's shooting to closure. Each passing week opened the door wider to speculation until it could no longer be closed.

Six months into the investigation, a 17-year-old black boy, Trayvon Benjamin Martin, was shot dead in Sanford, Florida, USA.

George Zimmerman, on neighbourhood watch duty for his gated community that evening, phoned the police to report a suspicious character he had spotted – a young black man wearing a hoodie. According to Zimmerman, he approached Martin, they had an altercation, and he shot him in self-defence.

When it turned out that Martin was not armed and was visiting his father's fiancée who lived in the gated community, my son expected justice to only go one way. But the police shot down such hopes by releasing Zimmerman with no charges. The police chief explained that there was no evidence to refute Zimmerman's claim of having acted in self-defence.

We wondered how the police would have handled the case had it been the other way round, and Martin had shot an unarmed Zimmerman in self-defence.

Protest marches across the US called for Zimmerman's arrest, and over 2 million signed an online petition for a full investigation and prosecution. Six weeks after the shooting, a special prosecutor appointed by the governor of Florida charged Zimmerman with murder.

### Reaction to verdicts

My son was a few months short of his 16th birthday when Zimmerman was acquitted of all charges. It took us both by surprise. We had both assumed that justice was as primed for change as the US political landscape.

But time still held US justice in custody. Laws punishing whites for crimes against blacks had historically been weakly enforced or easily avoided.

Justice wasn't ready to follow the lead of the colour-neutral presidency exemplified by the Obama administration. Outside looking in, it seemed events were daring Obama to be a black president.

My son welcomed the formation of the Black Lives Matter (BLM) movement in the US and kept abreast of the movement's campaigns against violence and systemic racism towards black people.

"What do you think of Black Lives Matter?" he sought my opinion.

"I support what the movement stands for. However, the inferred mandate is too broad. Detractors will have open season."

"In what way?"

"They could easily point out the movement isn't as vocal on black-on-black violence and other ills that affect black lives."

"I see it differently. The US police force is so well trained they only shoot as a last resort because life matters. However, statistics show there is less hesitancy to pull the trigger when black people face the end of the barrel. It's as if black lives actually do matter less."

Almost a month after his 17th birthday and nearly four years after the shooting in North London, an inquest jury concluded Duggan was lawfully killed.

Lowering his expectation of the entire justice system, he reflected, "It feels like this was the system's preferred verdict from the onset." Time elapsed and changing versions of what had happened eroded confidence in the outcome.

It opened the door for him to wonder whether there was a fairer justice system in Zimbabwe and other African countries. It turned out that on paper, the justice system was as good as any. But on the ground, there was evidence of erosion of the rule of law, mainly against political opponents.

Imperfect as the US and British justice systems were, most citizens of Africa considered them better than their own. This gagged African leaders from speaking out for the cause of descendants of the continent in western countries. It was, instead, Africa's diplomats who were often summoned over how their governments treated their own people.

What he found more painful to take in was the realisation that the machinery that kept the black majority oppressed during the colonial era was often left intact to serve a new privileged minority.

# NINE: CONNECTING WITH HIS ROOTS

I sensed my son getting drawn to his home country and Africa when he was as young as five. One evening on the way home from school, a glimpse into his inner world took me by surprise.

"Dad, are there black people from here, England?"

"What do you mean?"

"I asked a new black boy at school today where he was from, and he said he is English. Is that possible? I thought all black people are from Africa?"

I had some explaining to do. Then it was my turn to listen. A sense of belonging had become a big deal to him after feeling otherised in the only country he really knew. He couldn't reconcile how he felt with the illusion that anyone could belong anywhere, as sold by *Pocahontas*, one of his favourite animated movies.

Unlike him, his mother and I had already cemented where we belonged by the time we landed on British soil. So, we had been subconsciously living out of our mental suitcases, having deemed our time in England permanently temporary.

I, therefore, failed to anticipate what I could have predicted had I paid more attention. The right of residence only guaranteed conditional welcome. A true sense of belonging was not factored into the equation.

We briefly spoke about the home he didn't know, and I answered the few questions that popped up in his mind. I made a note to remember to set aside time for my wife and me to mentally unpack our baggage and start living in the present with him.

Our discussion must have been still fresh in his mind when I took him to bed. Pushing aside the book of bedtime stories I read him daily, he begged me, "Please tell me a story about Zimbabwe."

I resisted the temptation to rehash stories from my childhood that featured a witty hare, *Tsuro*, and a gullible baboon, *Gudo*. The essence could be lost in both context and translation, I thought.

Instead, I made one up on the fly about a boy his age, Boli, who, like him, was passionate about football. He lived in rural Zimbabwe and played his favourite game barefooted, often against booted players. Opponents learned to avoid the unforgettable Boli tackle. The story was about his exploits on the football pitch.

He immediately took to Boli and wanted to hear more about him every day for months. It daily stretched the imagination of the storyteller in me.

## Heritage

He became passionate about connecting to his roots in his early teens. But he first had to contend with the insinuation that

Africa's history started when Europeans came to the continent. It entailed some digging and, occasionally, some heavy lifting. It was just as well he had the stamina. I could only fill in the gaps.

He was fascinated to learn he could claim heritage to four great nations of Southern Africa, nations that transcended physical borders: the Shona, Zulu, Xhosa and Manyika.

He learned that his ancestors came from the northern regions of the continent at the peak of what historians called the Bantu migration. It gave the impression that the Bantu were a homogeneous people. But "Bantu" was most probably a collective term for "people."

The Swahili word for people is *watu*, and the Shona equivalent is *vanhu*. In Chinyanja, people are called *anthu*, and in Zulu and Xhosa, *abantu*. The so-called Bantu migration was a mass movement of different groups of people, each bound together by a common language, and shared values and beliefs.

His paternal grandfather's ancestors, the Shona, tracked south in search of suitable land for cultivation and the right climate. They settled in central and northern parts of modern-day Zimbabwe.

The Zulu, his paternal grandmother's ancestors, went further south and settled in present-day KwaZulu Natal, South Africa, where they built a powerful nation. Chief Lobengula later led a group that went north and settled in the southern parts of Zimbabwe and called themselves the Ndebele.

His maternal grandfather's ancestors, the Xhosa, settled in the present-day East and Western Cape of South Africa. A spirit of adventure led his great great grandfather to go north on his own. And he settled in the midlands of present-day Zimbabwe, where he eventually married and raised a family.

The Manyika, his maternal grandmother's people, settled in the east of Zimbabwe and parts of nearby western Mozambique. His grandmother's people were mainly in the Honde Valley.

The geographical positioning of his ancestors determined the subplots that shaped their history.

Though very little has been written about pre-colonial Africa, he observed that the essence of its history wasn't lost.

Whatever was worth remembering was passed on orally from one generation to the next. Names of people and places also narrated the history.

For instance, the city he was born, Harare, spoke of her ancient ruler, Chaminuka, who lived on top of the kopje overlooking the present-day city centre.

Chaminuka foresaw the coming of Europeans and warned his people, "A pale people with no knees (wearing trousers) are going to invade this land. They are too powerful for us to resist." Legend had it he hardly slept, *harare*, in Shona.

My son's research of ancient civilisations of the continent unearthed the Benin Kingdom and the Ghana Empire in West Africa, the Kingdom of Mapungubwe and the Kingdom of Zimbabwe in Southern Africa, and many others. He found out they practiced crop cultivation, kept cattle, mined gold, and traded with the Far East during their prime.

### Era of slavery

He came across snippets about the era of slavery all his life. There were reminders in movies, books, commemorations, and the aftermaths of the internationally sanctioned human rights abuse. He didn't dig into it until his late teenage years.

Among the first things he understood was that pre-colonial crop cultivation underwrote slavery. There would have been no African slave trade had the people been riddled with malnutrition.

"So, every slave ship sailed away with the strongest and the most productive, hey?" It was more an observation than a question.

"They also carried away hope, knowledge, and skill to the detriment of the local economy," I added.

In foreign lands, Africa's sons and daughters were forced to assume the burden of understanding instruction. They learned new languages and complex tasks on the job without formal training. And Africa's exiled also learned to live with state-sanctioned injustice. They were presumed guilty of craving freedom.

It was only in 1948 that the United Nations General Assembly adopted the Universal Declaration of Human Rights, which prohibited slavery in all its forms. But prohibiting slavery was one thing, eradicating it a different matter altogether. Africa's manpower remained exploitable.

## Setting the record straight

I arrived home one evening to an unusual situation – my son was excited about his Geography homework. For a few moments, I thought he had at last seen the light, and all that had gone before had been worthwhile – the persuasion, encouragement, incentives, lectures, shouting, threats, and withdrawal of privileges.

His Year 7 Geography teacher had asked the class to research and prepare presentations on any one of the seven wonders of the world.

Buzzing with excitement, he stated, "I am going to write about the Victoria Falls!"

I had never seen him that excited. So high was his motivation that he gladly skipped his favourite TV programmes to focus on the assignment. With no prompting or reminding, he just got on with the task. So, he completed it days before it was due. It was evident from the dry run that he had really done his homework.

"Anyone could be forgiven for thinking that if it hadn't been for David Livingstone, the Victoria Falls wouldn't be known."

"How will you set the record straight?"

"I'll tell the class we knew the majestic falls long before Europeans came to the continent. North of the river, they were called Mosi-oa-Tunya – which means 'the smoke that thunders'. And on the south side, we called them Mapopoma, which literally means 'waterfalls'."

The presentation turned out to be one of the highlights of the year for him, but the presumed love affair with Geography was short lived.

# TEN: MAKING SENSE OF THE COLONIAL ERA

### Raw facts

"Do people that romanticise the colonial era know the full facts?" he questioned after stumbling upon conflicting pictures.

He had gathered that from the 1880s, European powers invaded and claimed ownership of parts of Africa, raising the risk of conflict between invading nations. So, in 1884, the German government invited the main players and well-wishers to a conference in Berlin to formalise the process and bring about some kind of order.

The conference's main output was a political geography that had no regard for local culture or ethnic groups. People of the same extended family could find themselves on different sides of European-imposed borders. By 1914, most of Africa had been divided between seven European countries. Only Liberia and Ethiopia remained independent nations.

The next challenge was the occupation of the allocated regions.

No one expected a warm welcome. Africa neither knew nor would have endorsed the outcome of the conference.

The occupation of present-day Zimbabwe started in the 1880s with the arrival of Cecil John Rhodes and his British South Africa Company (BSAC). The company became the face of British occupation in Southern Africa.

The BSAC claimed that Chief Lobengula had given them mining rights in the whole of present-day Zimbabwe. But the chief was only the leader of the Ndebele who occupied the southern parts of the country. He had no jurisdiction over the whole region.

The Rudd Concession, signed in October 1888 and bearing Chief Lobengula's signature in the form of an X, gave exclusive mining rights to the BSAC as well as the power to defend this exclusivity by force, in return for weapons and an unspecified amount to be paid regularly.

One of the signatories, Charles Rudd, certified that he had fully interpreted and explained the document to Chief Lobengula. It wasn't clear if he was fluent in Zulu or if the burden of understanding was placed on the chief. What is indisputable was the chief's attempts to disown the agreement when he realised what he had signed up to.

"Would Zimbabwe's history be different if Chief Lobengula had not signed the Rudd Concession?"

"No. The Berlin Conference had already paved the way for British occupation of the region."

"So, what was the point of the Rudd Concession?"

"It served two purposes. They wanted an excuse, any excuse, to occupy the region, and secondly, to stoke tension between the Ndebele and the Shona – a classic divide-and-rule tactic."

"What for?"

"A divided people generally put up less resistance. Adding a civil war to the equation would have reduced scrutiny on the activities of the BSAC."

### Realities of the era

"Do you think colonisation was in any way beneficial to Zimbabwe or Africa?"

I should have anticipated he would eventually get to that juncture. As his initial thoughts were more important than my decades-old stance, I threw the question right back at him.

"I believe every perceived benefit of the era could have been attained without it."

There was no doubt he was on a collision course with commonly held notions. And the best he could expect from the many that held on to contrary perceptions was the agreement to disagree.

By then he had had enough practice at looking at things from all angles. Approaching it from a different side, he probed, "What was the worst of colonisation?"

It was tempting to be simplistic and confine it to just political and economic disenfranchisement, but there was nothing new I could tell him. He had long established that upon arrival in present-day Zimbabwe, the colonisers had found a land rich in natural resources and inhabited by self-sufficient land owners who grew crops and kept livestock. They claimed ownership to natural resources, drove the indigenous people off the most fertile and high-rainfall areas without any compensation, and crushed every revolt.

Spears were just no match for bullets. But guns were not the only weapons at their disposal. They could pass any legislation without opposition. The Land Apportionment Act (1930) formally divided land between blacks and whites. Based on population estimates of 1.1 million blacks and 50,000 whites, 49 million acres were set aside for whites and just 22 million for blacks.

Overpopulation in low rainfall and arid areas inevitably sank the black majority into poverty and created a conveyor belt of cheap labour in farms and growing towns.

So, "free" land, huge financial subsidies from the Rhodesian government and cheap labour saw white farmers dominate the country's agricultural sector. African agriculture, by contrast, was left to fend for itself on overcrowded and under-resourced lands.

From self-sufficient land owners, our people became servants and labourers. The historical injustice led to many uprisings and fuelled the fight for liberation in Zimbabwe.

His hunch that there was much more below the surface compelled me to give him pointers to what most radars failed to detect.

"Years of forced existence in survival mode was among the worst our people endured. We paid a high price for the lack of awareness of the long-term effects."

I wished I could assure him we had turned a corner, but we were still largely consumed with the here and now and hardly had room for medium- or long-term planning.

Consequently, we rarely built on the foundations of our predecessors, trapping ourselves in perpetual restarts. We didn't readily embrace the notion that ours wasn't the onus to complete every task, but to perfect what we could in the time we had before passing the torch to the next set of runners.

## Dismantling the past

"Why did it take more than 37 years to undo the outcome of the 1884 Berlin conference that lasted just three months?"

He had in mind the time lag between Ghana's independence in 1957 and the end of apartheid rule in South Africa in 1994.

"Different levels of economic interests dictated the pace. The more they stood to lose, the stiffer the resistance."

A white paper kickstarted the process that made Ghana the first country to extricate itself from colonial rule. But expressing similar aspirations in Zimbabwe, then Rhodesia, was an imprisonable offence. The leader of the last white minority government, Ian Douglas Smith, famously declared that not even in a thousand years did he see black rule in the country.

ZAPU and ZANU, led by Joshua Nkomo and Robert Mugabe, respectively, directed an armed struggle from bases in neighbouring Zambia and Mozambique. Over decades, the war claimed thousands of lives in combat, cross-fire, assassinations, and air raids.

A breakthrough came when the British Government hosted a conference at Lancaster House in London in 1979 to discuss and reach an agreement on the terms of an Independence Constitution and the holding of free and fair elections.

After three months of negotiations, the only stumbling block was land reform. Both ZAPU and ZANU had promised radical land reform upon gaining power during the liberation struggle and wanted an immediate redress of the land imbalance. More than

60% of the most fertile land was in the hands of white farmers who made up less than 2% of the population.

ZANU, led by Robert Mugabe, had rejected a proposal to wait ten years before instituting land reform. When the British and American governments offered to compensate white citizens for land after 10 years, Samora Machel, then president of Mozambique, pressured ZANU to accept the terms. Consequently, a fund was set up to operate from 1980 to 1990.

ZANU won the first free and fair elections in the country, and Robert Mugabe became the first Prime Minister of Zimbabwe in 1980. Everyone had reason to be optimistic.

### Foundation of hope

"What was it really like in Zimbabwe at the time of independence?"

A new dawn in the country had arrived with a pledge by the Prime Minister elect to abide by the terms of the Lancaster House Agreement. He called upon the nation to embrace national reconciliation, forget our grim past, forgive each other, and join hands in a new dispensation.

"There were celebrations almost everywhere. The country's exiled, war heroes, refugees, and academics, came back from different parts of the world. We had hope for a better tomorrow. The endgame for the majority in urban areas was a level playing field, but for rural Zimbabweans, it was land."

"What was your endgame, Dad?"

"Restoration of dignity, which demanded continuous reflection. I could, therefore, be a cheerleader one moment and a critic the next."

We hoped independence would make room for all of us on the grownups table, not just a privileged few.

"How was the call for national reconciliation received?"

"Extremely well by most us. It was the foundation of hope for a better tomorrow. It felt great to be Zimbabwean."

"How about the white community?"

"Only a minority rode the wave of hope. Most would not fully accept the new reality. Many left for neighbouring South Africa that was still under apartheid rule and others for destinations further afield."

"So, race was still a divider?"

"Oh yes. But it wasn't the only one. Tribal differences could also be exploited for political gain."

## Destabilising the foundation

"Why do you think the national reconciliation failed?"

"Partly because it wasn't homegrown. The main reason was the us-and-them culture that we were trapped in. It was just deep enough below the surface to be publicly deniable. Race, tribe, political party affiliation, and even liberation war credentials dwarfed real patriotism."

Looking back, it was apparent our peace pact was only as strong as our weakest points. But hope blinded most of us to how fragile it was. We had no awareness that one of the key points of the Lancaster House Agreement, regarding land, had sown the first seeds of division post-independence.

Reading in between the lines, it is apparent that the British Government prioritised the land ownership rights of white farmers above the resettlement of the landless, whilst the ZANU-led government had it the other way around.

Consequently, white farmers were more loyal to the British Government for safeguarding their interests. To compound matters, a large section of the white community still considered themselves Rhodesians.

That was just the tip of the iceberg. We paid a high price for staying a step or two behind pre-independence South Africa, who magnified tension between the Shona and the Ndebele using the same tactics they had employed in Angola and Mozambique.

The South African government supported and armed minority parties of newly independent states. They funded Mozambique's RENAMO against the ruling party, FRELIMO. In Angola, they threw their weight behind UNITA in a bitter war against the MPLA-led government. Then they covertly supported Super ZAPU to destabilise the ZANU-led government in Zimbabwe.

The bigger picture was a complex ideological war between the West and the East at the height of the Cold War. FRELIMO, MPLA and ZANU were deemed too close to Cuba and the Soviet Union for comfort. So, South Africa fronted the war against the spread of Communism and Marxism in the region.

Once conflict started, it set the irreversible into motion. Just two years into Zimbabwe's independence, rebels abducted and killed six tourists, two Americans, two Australians, and two Britons, on a safari near the Victoria Falls. The lives of these tourists, aged between 18 and 35, were traded for international awareness of political dissatisfaction with a democratically elected government.

"Was this common knowledge?"

"Only to people that wanted to know. Being half-Shona and half-Ndebele accorded me a ringside seat to the dynamics at play."

"What's your opinion of the massacre in Matabeleland?"

It looked like he was leaving no stone unturned. I hoped he would be able to separate the grain from most of the chaff in the public domain.

"It was a consequence of leadership failure. Super ZAPU was hoodwinked into believing a regime that kept Mandela locked up would have Zimbabwe's best interests at heart.

Both ZANU and ZAPU should have anticipated South Africa's moves following what had happened in Angola and Mozambique. But the government's reaction against its own citizens and ZAPU's apparent apathy played into the hands of the detractors. They were, therefore, both stripped of innocence and forced to cede moral high ground."

"If we couldn't rise above tribal politics, what hope did we have of building a multi-cultural nation?"

"Very little. Everything became shaky once the foundation was breached."

So, as a country, we only had ourselves to blame. We were not ready to unite to build on the huge potential we had. And the detractors only had to magnify existent divisions to derail us.

As it was easier to apportion blame than assume responsibility, we hung on to victimhood and drove with both eyes so firmly fixed on rear-view mirrors we hardly moved forward. It ruled out togetherness in tackling bigger issues like land reform.

### Land reform impasse

Land reform was carried forward from one to-do list to the next for 10 years, during which it was slowly downgraded from a national programme to a political party agenda.

The Zimbabwe Government was so confident the British Government would honour the Lancaster House Agreement they didn't panic after the agreed 10 years elapsed. Patience only dried up after seven more years went by without a word from the British. So, they tasked Kumbirai Kangai, then Minister of Agriculture, to craft a polite reminder.

Expectations of cordial government-to-government interactions quickly evaporated when they received a letter from Clare Short, then Secretary of State for International Development, in which she attempted to dissociate the Labour Party from Britain's colonial past and claimed her government had no special responsibility to meet the cost of land reform in Zimbabwe.

The response infuriated the ZANU government who had been persuaded in 1979 to honour the key obligations of the Rhodesian government that included paying pensions to military personnel they fought against during the liberation struggle.

Some in their ranks may have remembered the misgivings they had about putting off land reform for 10 years. Others may have felt empathy with Chief Lobengula's position a hundred years earlier.

"What was the real reason the British government pulled out of the agreement?"

"There was no money. Passing the bill to British taxpayers would have been political suicide for Labour."

"What about the fund set up to run from 1980 to 1990?"

"I don't think it ever existed."

"So, it wasn't just Labour that played ZANU?"

"No. I believe the British government thought they had shaken the monkey off their backs in 1980, and it had become ZANU's pest. So, they gambled that ZANU would not shoot itself in the foot whilst dealing with it."

Meanwhile, there was a growing divide between the grassroots of ZANU and the leadership over the major unfulfilled promise of independence: land. Putting it off any longer was tantamount to political suicide for Zimbabwe's President Mugabe.

Mugabe interpreted the British government's unilateral change of rules in the middle of the game as patronising and accused the Labour government of conducting themselves like colonial masters.

ZANU rejected the Labour government's offer to rewrite the land reform rulebook and decided to pen their own. So, politics robbed the people of Zimbabwe of the hope to orderly right a historical injustice.

In 2000, some twenty years after Zimbabwe's independence, the land impasse reached a boiling point. Upon receiving the green light from the ruling party, war veterans led and supported violent invasion of white-run farms. Chaos reigned as property got destroyed, and lives were lost.

The issue dominated international news channels and Zimbabwe government–controlled news outlets alike. Entitlement was the recurring theme, and justice hardly got a mention.

### Real costs of economic collapse

"From bread basket of Africa to basket case? What really brought down the economy? Sanctions or just incompetence?"

He hadn't quite appreciated how far the country's economy had fallen until he found out that between 1989 and 1991, Zimbabwe was one of only three countries in the world that exported more than they imported.

I sensed the enormity of the background issues my son was grappling with, top of which was the insinuation of inherent black incompetence. It didn't take much to figure out whose potential he was gauging and its implications. It called for straight answers with no sugar coating.

"It was two things, son, and neither had anything to do with our collective capability or potential. Our first mistake was to slap a price tag on self-sacrifice. It stripped our nation of its heroes."

He sat up, the wheels of his mind turning. Seeming to park his initial thoughts, he asked, "And the second?"

"We made entitlement our national anthem – entitlement to power, land and natural resources, with no accountability. The cocktail was lethal."

He quietly processed the information, nodding to himself, presumably as each piece fell into place. But there was more below the surface. The hidden tragedy was the live ammunition it handed detractors, which had some question the wisdom of ending white minority rule in the country and others imply that colonisation was motivated by the need to provide solutions to problems we didn't know we had.

I was, therefore, delighted when he enquired if we had the capability to guide our country back on track. At least he placed the responsibility of finding solutions in our own backyard, however littered it was with the debris of what could have been.

The worst times had seen us lose the one thing we couldn't make it without: trust. The dynamics of governing and being governed changed when trust reserves were bled dry. It was no secret that getting the country back on track hinged on rebuilding trust from the foundation up. We had everything else in place, including an abundance of natural resources, a smart people with a deep love for the country, and a positive work ethic.

Unfortunately, the influential saw a threat in every level playing field. So, they cultivated a culture of followership and criminalised leadership aspirations. The apparent dearth of leaders of the right calibre made boldness the primary attribute required to attract a following. So, trust remained elusive.

The mountain of data on Zimbabwe before him could not immediately provide answers to the most pressing question on his mind: what it said about him. I resisted the temptation to unpack it for him.

The penny dropped after a day or two. Appearing to have had a load off his back, he declared the situation in the country of his birth did not define who he was. Only he could.

# TWELVE: PASSING THE BATON

He calmed down when he finally realised that passing the baton wasn't an event but a process, and we had been at it for as long as he had lived. Much as it was his prerogative to choose the combination of options to run with, I was certain he could use all the help he didn't think he needed.

I was nonetheless aware of the risks. Alongside the good, I could unintentionally pass my flaws and prejudices, or worse still, saddle him with my own dreams.

So, I took every opportunity to reflect with him on the course my life had taken, where I had missed the mark, what I could have done better, and the lessons I'd learned.

By his late teens, I had confirmed his long-held suspicions that I wasn't infallible. Once he understood I was always going to be a work-in-progress, he embraced his own need for continuous learning.

How to make the most of both worlds was among the things he was forced to learn when it became apparent that fitting into either wasn't a given.

One school of thought made him an outsider in London because of where he was born, whilst another took him for a stranger in Harare because he was brought up elsewhere.

Fortunately, we had built enough trust reserves to enable us to jointly review every journey with the intended destination in mind.

### New law of the jungle

We noted that the law of the jungle had changed. The fittest were no longer in the driving seat however much they tried to hold on to this historical privilege. The new order only rewarded the readiness to adapt to continuously changing circumstances, elevating the smartest to the top of the food chain.

The majority convinced themselves they were for change. But what they had in mind was change on their terms – everything and everybody around them changing, but them. So, they almost always followed rather than lead or keep pace with it.

Embracing change entailed recognition that everyone was on the march, though some were on it reluctantly. He was, therefore, unlikely to meet the same person twice, as everyone was undergoing their own transformations, some for the better and others for worse.

Whilst no one unintentionally improved, no effort was required to degenerate. So, he was in danger whenever he slipped into effortlessness. Anticipation of and preparation for change were key to his daily survival.

Glory days gone by didn't count for much. The Shona adage "matakadya kare haanyaradze mwana" (a child cannot be fed on memories of a feast) was a permanent reminder to put the past in its rightful place and to get his priorities straight.

Communities were no longer built around outward appearance or physical proximity but bound together by a common outlook. As he had the privilege to choose his communities, he opted for global citizenship among others.

The new jungle was both a hunters' paradise and a living nightmare for the passive. Failure to learn from yesterday was rarely forgiven. Tables could be turned at any time without notice, and the hunter could just as easily become the hunted.

### Extended family

His first introduction to the extended family was almost coincidental. During his second visit to Zimbabwe, then aged 10, he thought the joke was on him when a young man almost twice his age called him uncle.

It kickstarted his education of the extended family tree, which could easily have been a study of database management systems. The attributes were identical: hierarchical, interconnected, and relational.

The family tree had all the hallmarks of a living organism. It grew in all directions from a network of roots that symbolised connectedness. Mutual accountability enabled it to withstand most storms of life.

Birth, marriage, and death were stages of life that were uniquely celebrated. Every birth brought fresh hope for a better tomorrow. Marriage could either be a blessing or a curse depending on whether it strengthened or stretched family bonds.

Once upon a time, death was only a one-way ticket into the spiritual realm. But the advent of HIV and AIDS turned it into a thief of potential.

At its best, the extended family offered protection and sanctuary to the vulnerable. But it wasn't without exploitable weaknesses that could allow entitlement to overtake mutual responsibility.

Despite its shortcomings, the extended family's positives far outweighed the negatives. Its support system averted disaster during the most trying times of our history, such as Zimbabwe's economic crisis. Many in the country would have been in dire straits had it not been for remittances from family members in neighbouring countries and abroad and the use of their assets.

He found it intriguing that parenting was culturally a collective effort. My brothers had fatherly responsibilities over him, and their children were his siblings. Equally, his mother's sisters considered him one of their own. In the ideal world of the extended family, real orphanage was non-existent.

When it dawned on him that his successes were mutually celebrated, and personal shame could bring disgrace to all, he sensed that accountability to the family was more daunting than standing before courts of law.

It taught him all the sides of love in a way nothing else could. The more he understood, the further he shifted away from the idea of love as a stagnant pond that only existed to be occasionally filled.

His picture changed to a vibrant river with multiple tributaries, a river that never dried up because every outflow triggered inflows from sources unknown.

## Making the most of the present

At the top of my regrets was the fact that I had never stood still long enough to take in contentment. Looking back, it was evident I could never hold on to it long enough, and on the rare occasions I somehow did, I only realised it in retrospect.

It was apparent that my son and I treated time differently. He could completely live in the present with no thought of what was to come, whilst I tended to put the present on hold in the hope of a future pay-off. The awareness of the need for balance at the back of my mind wasn't enough to bring it about.

Then I learned the true value of time from two near-strangers that were approaching the end of theirs. The last words of a pop star from my childhood, David Cassidy, were a timely reminder – "So much wasted time."

A family friend, a palliative care nurse, told me about her last conversation with a terminally ill lady, which left a lasting impression on me. Weakly holding our friend's hand, the lady whispered, "You know what I really wish for now?"

Without pausing, she explained, "To feel the rain on my face and the wind blowing through my hair."

Unfortunately, she didn't live long enough to see another day. Ironically, most Londoners consider a combination of wind and rain the makings of a terrible day.

Urging him not to leave any time unlived, I tried to undo every wrong signal I had given. We learned to appreciate the simple things in life that could easily be taken for granted: a place to live, a meal together, opportunity, hope, good health, freedom, belonging, and much more. We were surprised by our good fortune when we recounted everything we were grateful for.

### Celebrating ourselves

There was so much to celebrate within that it almost became a daily affair. We mentally stripped our continent of borders, claimed all icons with African roots as our own and celebrated their successes.

We were on our way home from a kickabout in a nearby park

one Saturday morning in the middle of the 2000 UEFA European Football Championship when a friendly neighbour asked my three-year-old which team he was supporting.

"France."

"France? You'd better have a very good reason."

He smiled but offered no explanation. At the back of his mind were Marcel Desailly, Patrick Vieira, and Zinedine Zidane, whose families were from Africa, and several of their teammates whose connection to Africa could be traced to slavery. His early heroes and heroines were in the limelight. So, it didn't take long for him to become familiar with the pain of many a hero's fall from grace.

The Black History Month was an annual reminder that the foundation of our celebrations couldn't just originate from victimhood. There were multiple lessons to be learned in sports, the arts, sciences, and other spheres of human endeavour. For instance, Venus and Serena Williams illustrated that only unforced errors stood in their way to tennis immortality. And their comebacks from seemingly hopeless situations were displays of resilience.

He noted that unforced errors of judgement, political and economic, were the root cause of distress in Africa. And closer home, it was essential he cut out unforced errors from his own life, because comebacks were not always easy to engineer for black boys.

## Top of the mountain

We had often spoken about the tragedy of reaching the top of the wrong mountain when he thought money was the solution to every problem. Part of him wanted to make a positive difference in people's lives, whilst the other hoped he would make an insane amount of money.

He had the aptitude to pursue a variety of careers and would have succeeded in anything he set his heart on. For a long time, he had his eye on the presidency of Zimbabwe. He then briefly considered pursuing law. At university, he first studied Business Information Systems before switching to Finance and Accounting. He thought he had compelling reasons to change direction each time.

The one consistent aspiration he had was first expressed in his mid-teens.

"I think I know what I really want to be above everything else – I just want to be a dad."

He then raised the bar of fatherhood much higher than mine. It made me think of everything I could have done better in raising him. I had no doubt he was headed in the right direction when I sensed his career goals had become only a means to an end.

In his late teens, he stated, "I want to have two or three children. And I want to be able to collect them from school daily just to spend time with them." I wished him well as I felt a twinge of guilt for prioritising food and shelter above time with him.

But time with my future grandchildren wasn't the only thing on his mind. After his 20th birthday, he told me, "I hope my children spend their earliest years in Zimbabwe before I take them anywhere. I want them to learn the language and the culture."

His hope for a better tomorrow assured me he was adequately armed to make everyone around him feel safe.

30441877R00064

Printed in Great
Britain
by Amazon